C0-CEG-880

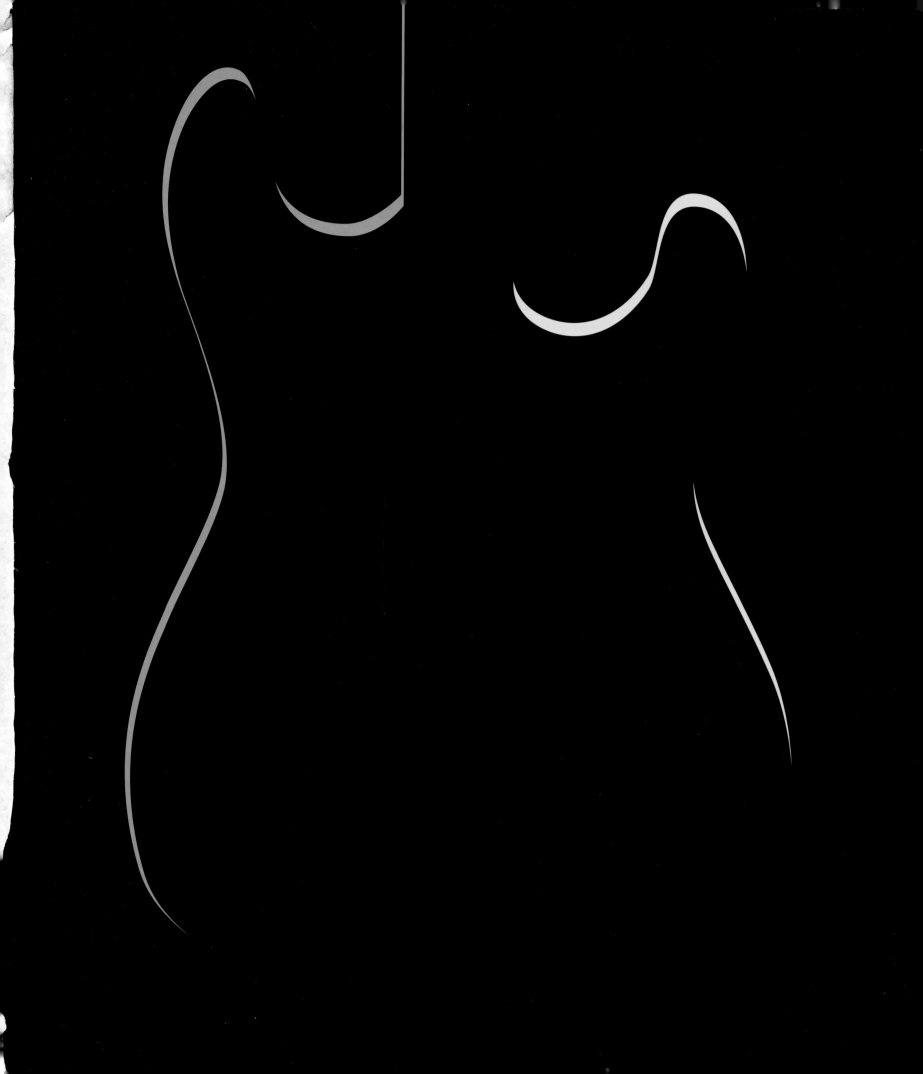

The Artists, Instruments, Myths and History of 50 Years of Youth Music

Ernesto Assante

LEGENDS OF ROCK

WHITE STAR PUBLISHERS

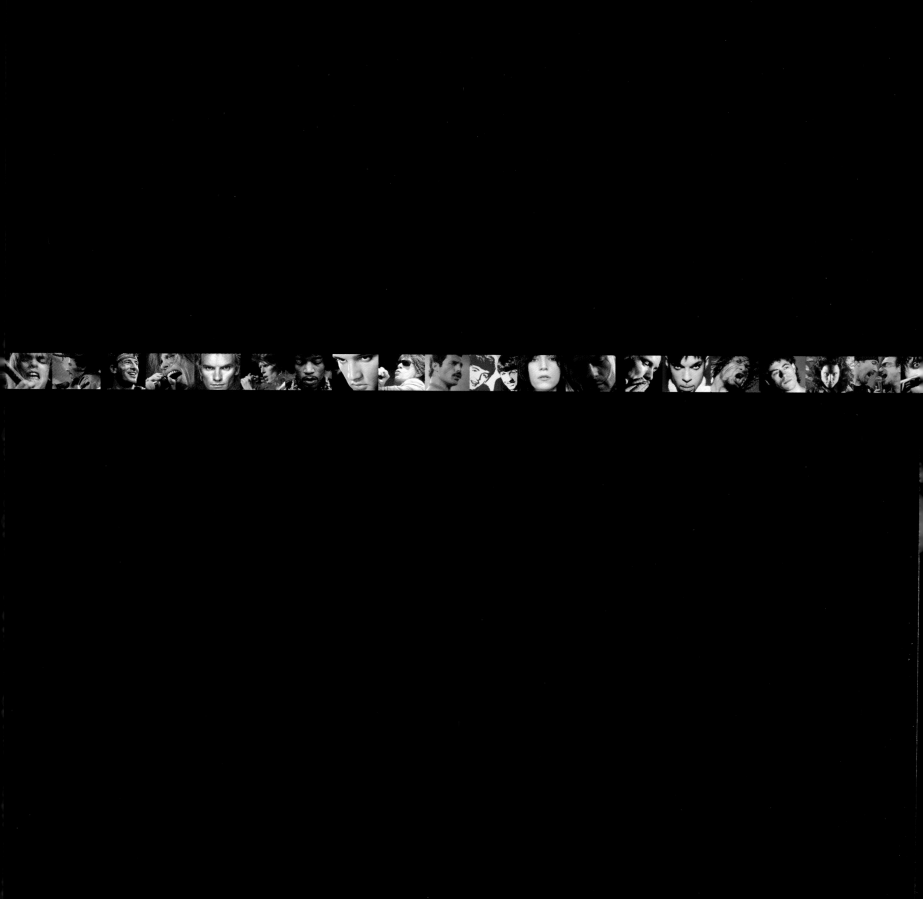

"This book is dedicated to Eleonora, Sofia and Costanza: what would life be without them"

TEXT BY

Ernesto Assante

editorial director **Valeria Manferto De Fabianis**

graphic designer **Clara Zanotti**

editorial coordinator **Laura Accomazzo**

CONTENTS

IF THERE'S ONE THING THAT MAKES ROCK DIFFERENT TO ALL OTHER MUSICAL GENRES, IT'S THE FACT THAT IT ISN'T A GENRE IN ITSELF.

At one point, in the late Sixties and early Seventies, rock conquered all, ranging right across the board and infiltrating almost every style of pop music. It rooted chiefly in the minds of the young as an attitude rather than a defined sound per se; it was a context in which to move. Within this context, in every era, styles of music and behavior have taken on meanings and sustained values that allow music itself to function as a medium for daily life. Consequently, in the young person's new scenario, each factor has its own value for communicating information, whether it be a motorbike, a haircut, a jacket, or a badge. Teenagers need to have dress and conduct codes so they can recognize one another and underscore their diversity: these are tools of communication that keep pace with music, which is a catalyst and a tool. These experiences are music that is "lived," basically, before it is listened or danced to.

Rock is the underpinning to the comprehension of recent history and current events, where the evolution of youth into a social subject is linked to the desire for freedom, intolerance for authority and a renewed interest in popular or esoteric cultures as "alternatives" to the status quo. Rock is the recovery of day-to-day life as seen through the lens of various unusual and startling forms of expression.

Beats, punks, hippies, rappers: rock has crossed and animated innumerable social and cultural movements; it has served as the soundtrack for changing times and seasons; it describes the world the way it is and how the young wish it could be; it inspires dreams and lifestyles for numerous generations, who have produced art and culture that left a decisive mark on the twentieth century.

Rock is a culture that enjoys the absolute privilege of notoriety, or rather, it exists precisely due to its popularity, because it is a mass phenomenon. We also have rock's mercurial and popular spirit to thank for the many social breakthroughs that slowly emerged in Western culture and went on to become collective heritage.

Rock and its 50 years in existence are an integral part of Western culture today: it is more of an attitude than a type of music; it is a way of seeing and considering the world and art. It is this aspect of rock's nature that allows it to blend and mix readily with other arts, from cinema to literature, painting to theatre. Rock transforms into a medium of mass communication, closely interlinked with radio, TV, and the Internet; it is an integral part of the universe of style and trends; it is the runaway train of political and social battles.

Elvis Presley, Fats D
Jerry Lee Lewis,
Richard, Buddy Hol
Big Bopper, Alan Fr
Vincent, Eddie Coo

omino, Chuck Berry
Bo Diddley, Little
, Platters, Bill Haley
ed, Les Paul, Gene
hrane, Ray Charles

50

A starting point would be to seek a sure date of birth and, in this case, seeking to apply any sort of "certainty" to rock 'n' roll would bring only the vaguest of results.

Versions, opinions, theories, regarding the birth of rock 'n' roll are many, too many to count, and all of them, whichever way we look at it, have some element of truth and are acceptable and substantially close what really occurred, and make some sense. In that case, we can't attribute the paternity of the genre to just one person and, equally, we can't define a specific date for the happy event. So, impartially and reasonably, we can state that rock 'n' roll was born in the mid-Fifties, between 1954 and 1956, thanks to many figures, who at the time were walking the fine line that separated not two but three different musical genres: pop, rhythm 'n' blues, and country. They were white and black musicians, folks from the Deep South and from the urban northeast, instrumental pros and callow youth, all looking for something, that special something, which could make real a sensation, a feeling, that couldn't be hidden any longer, that no one could now hold back.

What was it? It was "youth." Yeah, you say, youth has always been around, and each generation had its own, so?

But it wasn't that way, because youth as we know it today didn't exist then, and hadn't existed at all up to that time. You were a child, then you were an adolescent, then – like it or not – you were an adult. You wore a shirt and tie, you went to work (often you didn't even get to be grown up before you worked: children and especially adolescents worked). Then you started a family and you shouldered a whole lot of responsibility. In the post-war period, especially in the US, as victors of WWII and not forced to rebuild homes, industries and economies as were the Europeans, young people found themselves with money in their pockets, more time (they went to high school, not to work) on their hands, so the time span from being an adolescent to being an adult extended. They became the "young ones," the ones who now made up a unique new social category. So they wanted their own status symbols, their own language, and for the first time in history, they didn't want to be like their parents, they simply wanted to be "young." (Think of love, of sex, fun, and consumerism – other extraordinary novelties of the era).

And what did these young people need to be able to recognize one another? Just three things: T-shirts, jeans, and music.

At the time, "music" was, to a large extent, rhythm 'n' blues played by African-Americans, which gradually came out of the "race records" ghetto, and began to circulate amongst black and white American youth of the time. There's no doubt that Ray Charles was a hero in those days, someone who could speak the new language quicker and better than anyone else. Charles' music, like that of Ike Turner, Fats Domino, and many other Fifties soul men, was rhythm 'n' blues played by radio stations by hordes of new disc jockeys. It may have been aiming straight for the hearts of these kids, but the kids loaded it with a whole new meaning, seeing its sharp contrast with the music preferred by their parents. They danced to at parties to this music so they could hook up with the opposite sex – the music was "new" not so much in the sound but in the use. Alan Freed was a DJ broadcasting music to the kids and he tried to find a name for this new wave, so he called it rock 'n' roll and lined up all those making the right records: Little Richard, Jerry Lee Lewis, Buddy Holly, the great Chuck Berry.

None of them, however, earned the title of "father," or rather "king," of this new rock 'n' roll. That place was reserved for a Tennessee boy from Memphis: Elvis Aaron Presley. In the Sun Records studios he came up with an explosive blend of rock 'n' roll, which was a combination of rhythm 'n' blues, pop, and country, a mix of white and black sounds with which any kid could identify. He, like no other, succeeded in making rock 'n' roll important, embodying the music that was in the air, pointing the way for all the others, inventing a magic formula whose infinite variations are still casting a spell today.

In a few years, from 1954 to 1958, rock 'n' roll burned out its extraordinary energy, sent whole generations of musical entertainers to retirement homes, showed the world that the kids had arrived and that no way would they be leaving without a fight.

Then, from 1958 to 1960, recording companies tried to regain control of the situation, muzzling the most rebellious and dangerous rockers: Elvis served in the military for two years and the music, at least in part, changed its tune. But the pop renaissance wasn't to last long as the decade drew to a close and the Sixties arrived.

The Beatles, The Roll
Dylan, Jimi Hendrix, Fr
Janis Joplin, Kink
Velvet Underground,
Donovan, Faces, S
James Brown, San

JIMI HENDRIX
THE BEACH BOYS
FRANK ZAPPA
MICK JAGGER
THE BEATLES
THE DOORS
BOB DYLAN
THE WHO

ng Stones, Who, Bob

ank Zappa, The Doors

, The Beach Boys

he Band, Joan Baez

eve Winwood, Mc5

ana, Otis Redding

60

The scenario changed: gone were the United States and its highways, replaced by Britain, darker, rainy, small.

The Eden was no longer Hollywood or New York, but an English port called Liverpool, where four young men created the twentieth century's most extraordinary and legendary band: The Beatles. How difficult is it to imagine modern music without The Beatles? Rock and pop, singer-songwriters and even middle-of-the-road music were profoundly influenced by the art, music and attitude of John Lennon, Paul McCartney, Ringo Starr and George Harrison. They were the "Fab Four," the "Lads from Liverpool," as they were variously described during their providential and legendary career. They invented "Beat," and along with Bob Dylan, they were the forefathers of rock as we perceive it today. They wrote some of the loveliest and most famous songs of the last century and contributed to making youth "visible," they established new style rules, they made a whole generation grow their hair and do lots more besides. All in less than ten years, from 1962 to 1970, recording a dozen albums, all of which went down in the annals of history.

Beat changed the world. We're not kidding here: really changed it – forced a whole generation to change dress code, grow their hair, throw away the clothes handed down from parents and grandparents, dress in bright colors, tight trousers, mini-est of miniskirts. The youth that had begun to claim its existence through rock 'n' roll now demanded to be seen, to count, to exist. They wanted to decide not only what to wear or what to listen to, but also how to love and how to live. Beat was a revolution: in just a few years the world started turning at a different speed and music – all music – changed register. Apart from The Beatles, the most significant new arrival was The Rolling Stones, one of the most enduring and prolific groups on the world scene, and they were certainly the archetypal rock band as far as the public is concerned. Their enormous popularity was due to their unforgettable songs and riffs, Keith Richards' unique guitar and, above all, the voice and stage presence of Mick Jagger, not to mention the subversive image cultivated from the start, which stood in direct contrast to the more reassuring Beatles, and which has continued over the years, bringing unequaled financial success and fame.

Hot on the heels of these leaders were The Who, The Kinks, The Small Faces, and hundreds – nay, thousands – of other bands from all over the UK. Bands that overran the States, following the Liverpool Four: it was the "British invasion," and they descended on the US armed with guitars and songs that shook America, which was already on the move following the election of President Kennedy.

If it left the UK as "beat," after it got to the US, it turned into "rock." Rock, not rock 'n' roll, which was well in the past at this stage, many aspects quite forgotten, buried by the youthful energy of beat and the electrifying power of new groups, with their long hair and bright clothes. It was rock, and it wasn't just a musical genre any more: it was an attitude, a way of being, thinking, living, and, of course, writing and performing music. Rock, in other words, was a dream, a road, a model. A whole generation was doing the dreaming, one that after the beat explosion was trying to imagine a different world, a different type of relationship between human beings, between men and women, with society, trying to re-write the rules of daily life, of good manners, and customs. A generation which, first of all, was trying to illuminate itself, get into the spotlight and talk about itself, in a sort of great "reality show," without scripts and without stand-ins. Music, cinema, theater: all became tools for "live" narrative of what many young people the world over were feeling, inventing, what kids were doing or theorizing, what teenagers were trying to change, demolish, or revolutionize. Music, above all, became the main device for aggregation, turning into a flyer, a proclamation, but also a newspaper, a poem, a telegram for sending messages of all sorts all over the world.

Rock emerged almost by chance. To be precise, it arose from necessity because at the end of the day, it was impossible for it not to be. There were The Beatles, who had revolutionized the planet, there were the Beach Boys, who thrilled the US side of the pond, there were the sounds, the rhythms, the vibrations that had sown the seeds of the new reality. And there were the first of those young "rebels," James Dean and Marlon Brando, whose indelible images circulated the globe and are still powerful today. What the sounds, the rhythms, the vibrations, and the images were lacking was the "word," something that went a bit further than this rebellion "without a cause," that surpassed the simple, albeit seminal, revolution brought by Brit beat.

The "words" came from a young man called Robert Zimmerman but better known as Bob Dylan. He breathed life into rock as such, his were the words that offered rock a soul, he gave some sense to the buzz of a generation that was already on the move. It didn't take much, really, to free, once and for all, the bodies, brains, and souls, and put together the most explosive musical mix of the century.

Rock was not born as a genre: how could Dylan's "Like a Rolling Stone" and the Kinks' "You Really Got Me" possibly be part of the same family? True enough, the sounds are light years away from one another, just as Dylan's vocal style, to quote another example, really has little in common with that of The Who's Roger Daltrey. Yet The Who, Dylan, Donovan, The Kinks, even The Beach Boys, really did speak the same language, and it was the same as that spoken by kids on either side of the ocean, the rock kids, the same spoken by Californian hippies and English Mods, the same that allowed New Yorker yippies to be perfectly in tune with the French worker-student action committees. The language of rock, unique and copious at the same time, a language embracing beat, surf, blues, country, folk, exotic and oriental elements, electrification, and improvisation, quickly became the planetary and global language. Rock became the banner under which to recognize others and identify yourself, with which to highlight your diversity, your refusal of middle-class rules, the world of parents and outdated institutions. The decade that The Beatles and Rolling Stones had turned upside down, was further revolutionized by the advent of rock and of a generation that was no longer going to make do with simple beat rituals, but aspired to changing the world. Jim Morrison and The Doors were soon to sing "we want the world and we want it now," opening the gates, once and for all, to a total and absolute utopia.

Rock brought, therefore, increasingly different colors, moods, tastes, and rhythms, with a thousand faces and a thousand sounds, and continued from that moment on to be a magnificent and legendary melting pot where everything and the opposite of everything had its legitimate place. There was Dylan and his "Like a Rolling Stone," an outright manifesto of this new music, a song that on its own stood for the sentiments and sensations of a generation on the move, seeking new voices to express itself and the world of which it dreams. There was The Band, with Dylan and without him, writing legendary pages of Sixties and Seventies American musical history, dipping deep into tradition and looking ahead with self-assurance and originality. Sounds and words that when compared to Pink Floyd's "Atom Heart Mother" seem a million miles away: at that time Pink Floyd were exploring the roads of psychedelia, seeking to extend the boundaries of rock in an extraordinary way, as we can see in tracks like "Set the Control For the Heart of the Sun." Experimentation, like that pursued by Pink Floyd, was occurring in a UK that had recovered from its beat hangover and was laying down the law for new music with the legendary band The Who (a group that went so far as to compose a rock opera like *Tommy*, destined to leave a permanent mark on the development of rock in the years that followed), with the Davies brothers' Kinks, expert performers of riffs that became classics, like "You Really Got Me," or memorable songs of the caliber of "Sunny Afternoon."

The Who, above all, are worth looking at: a quartet of very young London Mods who cut their first single in 1964. It was July 3 and the group was then called The High Numbers. The single's two songs were "Zoot Suit" and "I'm the Face." The band had already changed names once, from The Detours, and the new name it soon coined, The Who, was quite unique and brought them luck, taking them into the annals of history. Forty years is pretty good for a band whose most famous single, "My Generation," stated " hope I die before I get old." Roger Daltrey, the group's vocalist, still sings that amazing refrain with the guitarist, composer, and soul of the band, Pete Townshend, but the other two original group members of the Brit band, drummer Keith Moon and bass player John Entwistle, have both died. Moon OD'd on drugs and drink on September 7, 1978; Entwistle died June 27, 2002, in a Las Vegas hotel, said to have consumed too much cocaine. Certainly, The Who laid some of the milestones of the twentieth century's pop and rock history, traveling through four decades without their legend rusting with the passing of time. Champions of the Sixties "Brit invasion," kings of planetary rock in the subsequent decade, putative fathers of the punk generation, The Who wrote songs like "My Generation," "Behind Blue Eyes," "The Kids Are Alright," "See Me, Feel Me," "Pinball Wizard," to mention but a few, and which are now considered true rock classics on par with songs by The Beatles, The Stones, and Bob Dylan. The band wrote two rock operas, *Tommy* in 1969, and *Quadrophenia* in 1973, which have been produced in numerous film and stage versions. They sold something like 100,000,000 discs and even now their albums, at every re-issue, will attract new and old admirers ready to grab them up.

We've already mentioned The Doors, who took rock to the limits of drama and poetry, and let's not forget Janis Joplin, who tore up the roots of the blues to transpose them into the new language of youth. Shouldn't we now mention the greatest guitarist in the history of rock, Jimi Hendrix? His musical career lasted three short years, from 1967, when he cut his first record, to 1970, when he died of an overdose in London. Three years, enough time for him to turn the vocabulary of rock back to front, inspired by blues, which underpinned all his music, and taking rock to a higher plane of complexity and expression. With Hendrix, the guitar became rock's leading instrument: a fetish to adore, the magic key that would unlock doors that had been until then sealed tight shut. Hendrix flew higher than anyone else, and burned out fast, along with an entire generation that dreamed and sped without heeding obstacles in its path.

This multicolored, multiform world of Sixties rock was the stage for hundreds of bands that rode its highways with different sounds and ideas, with enormous success and equally enormous surprises. Rock that ranged from Julie Driscoll and Brian Auger's flirting with black music, scaling the charts with "Save Me," to Donovan's ephemeral psychedelic folk (such as his classic "Mellow Yellow"), or Van Morrison who left the band Them to focus on his own poetic music, or Rod Stewart who left The Faces and tried to make some sense of the English rock wobbling between pop and soul, or the magnificent Troggs and their "Wild Thing," or the marvelous Frank Zappa, who unhinged rock itself by mixing it with jazz, classical and avant-garde music tempered with pop and blues, and added a touch of vaudeville and mockery. There are also the fascinating stories of figures like Steve Winwood, who forsook the Soul of the Spencer Davis Group to found the progressive Traffic ("Dear Mr. Fantasy" is one of British rock's great classics), and that of The Beach Boys, who were present at the dawn of the Sixties, riding the crest of the surf wave, and then shrugged off their goody-goody image to compete with The Beatles for the scepter of the "kings" of the new music. The Sixties, as we said at the start, changed the world. The entire world. In Italy the decade spawned hundreds of rock bands, and in France a rock legend was born: Johnny Halliday, who could translate rock' n' roll classics and for the first time the sentiments of youth were expressed through modern, electric music, with an exciting rebel attitude. At the end of the day, it was all rock, with all its theories, destined to change the horizons of popular music for many years to come.

There came the time, afterwards, when the Hippies appeared on this horizon: kids whose hair grew even longer than their big brothers, who left their families to go and live in communes together with other kids who believed in free love, preferring barter to money, imagining a world that really was different in every single way. They were "flower children" and they proclaimed, of course, "flower power." They wanted an end to war in Vietnam and they decided that California was the "promised land." The Californian bands, based in San Francisco, began to play the movement's music: Jefferson Airplane and The Grateful Dead were the first to shift the sound of rock towards psychedelia, revising the catalog of sounds and clothing, staging an out-and-out revolution. This was the phenomenon (followed by that of Abbie Hoffman and Jerry Rubin's Yippies, the more political wing of the movement) that spawned an alternative generation who practiced utopia for a few years, even celebrating their own nation for three days at Woodstock, in 1969, apex and conclusion of the first, historic and legendary, phase of rock, when half a million young people self-managed themselves to achieve the dream of a different, very very different life.

Then **THE SEVENTIES** came and the movement imploded. Utopias were stored in closets, and reality, with all its drama and pain, came back to the spotlight. Which was when THE SINGER-SONGWRITERS ARRIVED.

JIMI HENDRIX, 1967 ◀
The famous guitarist before a concert.

THE BEATLES, 1963 ▲
The British group appearing on the Ken Dodd Show
in 1963.

1964

BOB DYLAN

The Times They Are A-Changin'

1965

THE WHO

The Who Sings My Generation

1965

BOB DYLAN

Higway 61 Revisited

1966

THE MOTHERS
OF INVENTION

Freak Out!

1967

THE BEATLES

Sgt Pepper's Lonely Hearts
Club Band

1966

THE BYRDS

Fifth Dimension

1966

THE BEACH BOYS

Pet Sounds

1966

THE DOORS

The Doors

1966

JIMI HENDRIX
EXPERIENCE

Are You Experienced

1967

PINK FLOYD

The Piper At The Gates Of
Dawn

1968

JEFFERSON AIRPLANE

Crown of creation

1968

VAN MORRISON

Astral Weeks

1966

JIMI HENDRIX
EXPERIENCE

Electric Ladyland

1969

CROSBY, STILLS AND
NASH

Crosby, Stills and Nash

1969

FRANK ZAPPA

Hot rats

1969

THE BEATLES

Abbey Road

1969

NEIL YOUNG

Everybody knows this is
nowhere

1969

THE ROLLING STONES

Let it bleed

1969

THE WHO

Tommy the who

1969

THE DOORS

Absolutely live

Pink Floyd, Eagles, K
Jethro Tull, Yes, Dav
Kiss, Crosby Stills
Simon & Garfunkel
Mitchell, Sex Pistol.
Elton John, Roxy M
Deep Purple, Kra

BOB MARLEY
THE ROLLING STONES
JOHNNY ROTTEN
DAVID BOWIE
JIMMY PAGE
FREDDY MERCURY
PATTI SMITH
BRUCE SPRINGSTEEN

ng Crimson, Genesis
d Bowie, Marc Bolan
& Nash, Neil Young
James Taylor, Joni
, Clash, Patti Smith
sic, Black Sabbath
twerk, Areosmith

70

ROCK, by its very nature, cannot be too easily classified.

Of course, over the years countless labels have been coined to try and create some order in the immense sea of styles that defy inclusion in a single category. Critics and fans, enthusiasts and the public at large, as well as the young generations taking their turn on the stages of the world, have appropriated the language of rock and defined a truly endless series of sub-genres, many of which describe some novelty or other, while many others refer to no more than a look, a dress code, an attitude, or a social or cultural group that wanted to be part of rock but simultaneously wanted to be different from the "others." So there are many "rocks" – a great many, in fact, and several can be defined musically as rock only by an extreme stretch of the imagination, but even these have some inherent personal creativity. Can the musical family of "grandpa" Elvis Presley be related to – let's pinpoint any one of many of the latest generations most famous groups – Metallica? Yes, it can, and the relationship is in the attitude, in the way of relating to music, the way in which the authors, although decades apart, despite the differences in writing and playing, notwithstanding conflicting styles, handle the raw material of their musical profession. In other words, it's all about the song.

A lengthy essay – a whole encyclopedia – could be written on the "rock song," exploring its depths, its development, evolutions, changes, revolutions, starting with Elvis, of course, and continuing through the years to the present day. Wouldn't that be a fascinating study? It wouldn't be difficult to discover that today's song, whether it's a pop song, or a dance hit, or one written by a singer-songwriter, or a soul hit, owes a debt to the rock song, to the way in which rock dealt with the form itself: the traditional development of verses and refrains, the actual way a singer sings, the relationship with the lyrics and the stories told. Without rock we wouldn't have most of today's songs, or rather, these songs would be extremely different. Rock offered songs a freedom of expression that they did not enjoy previously, it broke down rules that for decades were undisputed, almost carved in stone, and gave singers some previously unknown tools for interpreting music: the first being the singer's own body movement, because in rock the body often "sings" alongside the voice. There are countless other examples.

The fathers of this modern relationship with song are, of course, The Beatles, but a great many who came after practiced the difficult art of song, enriching the catalog of sounds, colors, and emotions that each artist has available. The most extraordinary period of the rock song was certainly between the Sixties and Seventies after the beat hangover passed, and rock composers to some extent rediscovered the song form. They didn't, however, return to the canons of the past, but re-read the song format through in light of what they had learned, freeing their own creativity to experiment freely with different theories.

A foil for singer-songwriters, who came chiefly from America, like Paul Simon or Jackson Browne, or Canada, like Joni Mitchell and Neil Young, emerged in Britain: progressive music was born.

It may be coincidental, but while the Sixties revival began and never ended, while the music and styles of the Eighties are still flourishing (and soon we'll be in the full flush of the inevitable Nineties revival), recollections of the Seventies, taken as a complete lavish decade, tend to recede.

Certainly, the anniversaries of disco music, or punk, are happily celebrated, and there is always tendency for fashion to drift back to platform shoes and bell bottom pants, or long hair and flowery T-shirts, but each time the trend is for a partial revival of the decade, of a particular image from those glorious, awesome ten years, a sound, a fashion: there is no mention of the Seventies as a whole. Nor is it a coincidence, simply because it is actually impossible to celebrate, in substance, the revival of a decade that was many decades rolled into one.

First, there were the Seventies that were the extension of a previous decade, given that the attitudes and beliefs of the Sixties resounded throughout the Seventies – even if, and this must be said, the influence was decidedly stronger and longer-lasting in the American context than in the British context. Hippyism was declared "officially" dead in 1967, but was far from defunct, the distant communes born in the heart of Haight-Ashbury, continued with their lives, alternative "families" carried on the dream of a different society, one that was better, more free, and more open, for the entire first part of the decade. The "movement," more political and challenging, undoubtedly experienced a reappraisal phase, a resurgence, but the pacifist battle did not stop at the end of the Sixties: it actually continued vigorously for the early years of the new decade. So, in point of fact, no one cut their hair or put away their joints, and rock, which had been substantially alternative music until the end of the decade (apart from the great success of the more famous groups and solo artists), slowly turned into mainstream music, modifying deep down the structure of the actual record industry. However, in the early years of the decade, pop was standing up well – extremely well – to the onslaught of rock, and while it adapted to the times, continued to churn out successes. Up to 1973-74, actually, the Sixties echo continued to resound, even if, in many aspects the previous decade's "revolutionary" message was sugar-coated, commercialized, popularized, rendered harmless, in many cases reduced to an image with little or no substance.

Musically speaking, the "glare" of the Sixties lasted a much shorter time. If the Sixties rock revolution established itself on the cultural front, in the early Seventies it really became a planetary mass language. This was musically evident as early as the end of 1969, when on each side of the Atlantic, music took a different road from those which dominated the actual Sixties. For better or for worse, Woodstock was a watershed, a turning point. First of all because the record industry became aware of the potential of rock as a mainstream phenomenon, of the possibilities the music had in what was no longer a niche, but instead a colossal and planetary market, and rock, in the shortest time, changed its skin and went from being the banner of the counterculture to being a corporate and commercial business, while still somehow retaining its links with a fast-changing youth culture. Then the music makers realized that they had a wider range of possibilities than the three-minute song, albums ceased to be collections of singles and became receptacles of more extensive projects, vaster thoughts, more complete bodies of work.

The new arrival was called "progressive" rock and, especially in Europe, rock sought inspiration from high culture, like classical music, jazz, and improvisation.

Here we find the Seventies of progressive music starting at the end of the Sixties and continuing to the middle of the decade, involving millions of listeners all over the world, mixing the vestiges of hippyism with a new cult of personality, zealous soloism, superlatively fine technique, and a spectacularity that often, especially in later years, became an end unto itself. In this creative arena, rock abandoned its links with its roots, it transformed, renewed, changed its skin and its soul, reached its creative limits and at the same time was all too often reduced to being a mere formula.

Then with an extremely important aspect of the Seventies, the singer-songwriters, came, bearing the renewal of the song. Music was entrusted to the able hands of a number of wonderful composers and performers who shrugged off the garb of prophets of a youth culture on the move and attempted to describe private and personal sentiments, that nevertheless remain collective.

So, what about rock? The strong, electric, combative, extraordinary collector of dreams and needs, emotions and passions? No, it hadn't died. If anything, in the southern states of America it had become stronger and more creative, mixing with the blues and with improvisation, in a subgenre referred to as "southern rock" driven by electricity and dreams, but this was no longer a collective language, a generational flag. Then came glam rock, originated by one of the greatest artists ever known on the British rock scene, David Bowie. We shouldn't forget German electronic avant-garde either, or the experiments with jazz rock, disco music, funk and so many other styles – too many to mention. Except for one kid, who came from New Jersey, played the guitar, wrote and sang his own songs and believed he was

"Born to Run," the 1975 song that made Bruce Springsteen the new king of rock, a role that he has no trouble playing even now. Springsteen revived the hard, pure rock dream, describing deepest America, the passions and desires of a generation on the move with simple, direct language, presenting himself and his growth without fictions, preaching the rock word with unimpeachablee passion.

Nor should we overlook Seventies punk, which revolutionized everything and overturned the fine table where the rock stars sat at banquet, away from everyday life, their public, their kids, their true desires, and their real stories.

Nonetheless, the Seventies are more than all this: there are a great many figures whose records and innovations left their mark on the decade. Often, bands and individuals had begun their evolution in the previous decade and found their true voice in the Seventies.

The decade's strongest memory is linked, however, to progressive rock. So, what is this progressive rock? Can it really be given a definition? Let's hear Scaruffi, whose *Storia del rock* (*Story of Rock*, published in Italian by Arcana) sketches out the essential lines of the birth of the genre in the UK:

The extinction of beat, in about 1966, brought other musical types to the limelight, including the various revivals and psychedelia, none of which had the necessary charisma, however, for taking a lead in British rock. The dismemberment of British rock into parallel phenomena did lead to the exploration of areas miles away from rock and roll or beat, with a consequent rediscovery of blues, folk, jazz, classical music. These mixed elements converged, towards the end of the Sixties, into a genre that respected artistic merit rather than commercial success, a kind of music that required the listener to savor the components and the architecture. The melody was the "bond" rather than a center of gravity. Often, arrangements or progression counted more than a refrain.

Scaruffi has offered a faithful and precise overview. Let's try to add the "socio-political" nuance, which is of no little weight. At the end of the Sixties the revolutionary drive that had emerged in France and Italy caused the birth of a strong political youth movement, but in the UK this was not the case. Without doubt, there was a revolutionary British Left rooted in youth culture, but on the whole this movement did not follow the libertarian line of the French protests of May '68, preferring a quite different form of intellectual research. British youth did not protest in public, it imitated Californian colleagues and attempted to practice a revised lifestyle, to experience art in a new way. They did not conceive changing the system: quite the opposite, they lived the defeat of the American "movement" as a personal failure. Songs changed: clear, direct themes were forsaken for flights to wistful shores, unreal worlds, towards a free, creative universe that did not exist before. Rock destroyed the barriers once and for all, moving freely and fearlessly into combinations that were previously unthinkable, crossing the border into jazz with extreme self-assurance, breathing life into unique and fascinating musical forms, seeking to make its own the pleasure of composing, gathering in full from cultured music, plunging headfirst into the avant-garde and electronic research, and playing with technology with increasing strength and conviction.

ROCK was basically evolving, to the point that it was no longer recognizable,

eventually changing its very nature, although it never betrayed its initial approach. No – we must backtrack here. Perhaps there was a total betrayal of some aspects: if rock 'n' roll, hippy beat, and rock had preached and practiced sexual freedom, a new relationship with the body, progressive rock was conversely asking the audience to stay still, even quite often to sit down, to listen during concerts and to look (with progressively more sophisticated scenic devices and increasingly enthralling light shows) without moving. It's a distinction that wasn't exactly small, if we recall that the primary drive behind the entire rock revolution was Elvis and his gyrating hips.

The comparison with Elvis is significant not just in physical and sexual terms. What does the music of Elvis have in common with that of a band like Soft Machine, for example? Nothing, frankly. The music heard made by a fine, innovative band from a CD like *Five* is light years away from Presley, with no apparent connection whatsoever, direct or indirect, in terms of style and sound. So what keeps both types of music together under the rock label? It's in the approach, the way the musicians tackle the music, the field that has been chosen, which is not that of intellectual music nor that of African-American jazz, despite the strong bonds. Instead the approach is that of new popular music – rock, of course – that intrepidly mixes high and low, composition and improvisation, youth culture and spiritual exploration.

Moreover, this was also a time of new technological revolutions, which brought possibilities of increasingly sophisticated results from recording studios. During most of the Sixties, recorded music was a faithful reproduction of what a band was capable of offering live on stage, but gradually records began to be totally different items, assuming a crucial role in the artist's career, no longer as simply a means to an end but often the end itself, the scope of artistic creation. Recording technologies rapidly grew in sophistication and early-Sixties mono recordings were first replaced by stereo, then by 4-, 8-, and 16-track recordings. Consequently, groups could record a song one instrument at a time, separately, so it was almost natural that the "collective" creative underpinning to the previous decade's rock was relegated to a secondary role. On the other hand, it was precisely the decade's music to provide space (far more than Sixties rock had ever done), for creative improvisation, so that live music never resembled what was recorded.

1

3

1. A portrait of Joni Mitchell, 1968.

2. Bruce Springsteen and Jackson Browne, New York, 1979.

3. David Bowie-Ziggy Stardust in the USA, 1972.

When we hear "progressive," we immediately think of long suites played by musicians that feel like interminable solos, complex structures that are difficult to understand at first impact, where classical music and jazz, rock and improvisation, tradition and futurism mingle.

Yes, it's true, that progressive music was partly this, and actually this part of progressive music was what generated the most extraordinary and original results, which still trigger a little apprehension in today's musicians. However, we shouldn't forget that progressive music was also the creative space in which some extremely odd and unique songs were written. Real songs, with a melody, a verse, and a refrain, and peculiar songs, strange, different from the usual stuff, songs that magnificently withstood the tests of time and whose beauty has survived intact to the present day.

Difficult to believe? Well, look at Emerson, Lake & Palmer. The first thing that comes to mind is *Tarkus*, the fantastic re-reading of Mussorgsky's *Pictures at an Exhibition*, we recall Keith Emerson and his knife-sharp keyboards (yes, really sharp) at the key moments during their live concerts, but we really recall one of their loveliest, and most fortunate songs, "Lucky Man," a tiny jewel of prog rock mixed into song.

We could even mention Yes and feel a wave of progressive boredom, from the triple albums (the interminable *Tales from Topographic Ocean*), from the spectacular ability of the British group's individual members, from late-Seventies shows full of smoke and light but without many ideas. We forget that Anderson and his partners were, above all, a rock band, able to dictate the rules of fusion between song and progressive in albums like *Yes Album* and *Fragile* (two albums of that standard in just eight months – those were times of unbridled and fantastic creativity), and of writing irregular, marvelous songs like "Roundabout."

OK, you might say, then where is the charm, the romanticism, where are the touching and galvanizing words, where is the art of the word that made the rock song great, more often than not, by dipping into poetry? It's all there, concealed amongst the folds of work by Wyatt and McCormick's Matching Mole, in songs of splendid, striking beauty like "Oh Caroline," which proves that love, the true sort, can be so in 1001 different ways, and even the most militant, original, creative and innovative of the progressive bands, like Matching Mole, were quite capable of talking of love and composing memorable melodies.

Then, if we really want to talk about lyrics, we should try reading "Killer" by Van Der Graaf Generator, and see how Peter Hammill managed to put together poeticism and sound exploration while remaining a singer-songwriter (which is what he really was) and merging his songs into the music of his mates, creating a form of progressive rock that is still to be surpassed.

If we want to remember progressive art that was nevertheless, real rock, we might recall Ian Anderson's Jethro Tull, capable of writing astonishing suites like *Thick as a Brick* and at the same time coining a riff destined to go down in the history of rock, like "Aqualung." Such perfect examples of progressive rock, still not confined to its own rules, and aware, at the end of the Sixties, that it was speaking the world's electric language.

So, not just music, not just technique, not just the taste for exploration, for co-mingling of genres, not just the dream of a kind of rock that wants to become cultured and mature. The progressive proposed in this record still contains the delight in song, in melody, for it's a song that, despite everything, was still extremely singable and was able to tell a story.

Of course we don't want to say that this is all there was to prog rock; quite the contrary. It was the wealth of hypothesis emerging from the progressive scene to allow today's listener to understand how all these elements, songs and experiments, were experienced by the public as a single thing, as "rock" and nothing more, like a shared language that everyone, really, was able to comprehend and speak. It may feel strange, even absurd, imagining the Sixties and Seventies rock audience raving over groups like Soft Machine, whose "All White" filled clubs all over Europe. It may seem odd that bands like Curved Air had a respectable following and that their vocalist, Sonja Cristina, was considered a great sex symbol at the time, despite the band's music being quite removed from any sort of sexual temptation. Yet the reality was that of exceptionally open-minded musicians and audiences curious about all new possibilities.

Well, it was possible to pass from hard to prog rock, from glam to experimentation on the knife-edge of jazz, from electronic to melody, without much trouble. Which meant that musicians enjoyed quite a lot of freedom, and one of those who exploited this freedom to the full was Brian Eno.

A great deal of today's music owes something to Brian Eno. He was the quintessential "non-musician," yet the most significant musician of our times for popular music. For someone who, at the end of the day, didn't really "play" anything at all, he still pointed an entire generation in the direction of what and how to play. Today there isn't a disc or an artist that, consciously or not, hasn't been inspired by one of his theories or, even more than that, by some sound invention or innovation of his. Skeptical? Well, think about this: all the music that came from behind the fascinating "Buddha Bar" logo owes him something. The entire art of sampling is indebted to him, as is rock after Talking Heads, Devo, and, especially, U2. Innovation, realized with Eno, sounds quite radically different today, and even dance, and electronic, have learned the Eno lesson. Yes, because Brian Baptiste St. George de la Salle Eno has been on the music industry stage since the early Seventies: as a musician with Roxy Music; as a composer for the entire "ambient" scene; as a producer for U2; as a rocker in his own right; and as a musical thinker, leaving an indelible mark on contemporary, popular and avant-garde music, realizing highly significant records from a theoretical standpoint (like, for instance, *My Life in the Bush of Ghosts* with David Byrne, or *Music for Airports* as a solo artist) and extremely successful albums as a producer (from *Remain in Light* for Talking Heads to U2's *The Joshua Tree*).

Since the late Seventies, Eno stopped his performing in public and focused only on working in the studio. At the time of writing he has not given any further live performances; he prefers to sit at the mixing board or release his legendary installations, preferring to compose rather than appear. From the end of the Seventies to 2005, he recorded no real song (except for a collaboration with John Cale and in the bizarre adventure with U2, called "Passengers") written, sung, and played himself. So, if it's true that life goes on changing all the time, then Brian Eno has made this a rule of his art, rebuffing set formulas and encoded patterns, right from the start of his career with Roxy Music, where he practiced the art of noise with electronic machinery, passing through the most diverse experiences, always seeking new solutions, often pointing out new paths. He was also the name behind several of the Eighties and Nineties liveliest "trends," including electronic pop, "de-evolved" music, no-wave, electrofunk, the rediscovery of African music, and ambient-music, never failing to apply his extremely personal work method.

There are many more stories, theories, songs from the Seventies and if we felt like doing something nearly impossible, like selecting the ten songs that contributed to defining rock as a genre and as a culture, we'd have to include Velvet Underground's "I'm Waiting for the Man." First of all because, musically speaking, the song, written back in 1967 (when most of the rock world had other things on its mind: flowers, peace, love, especially in the legendary summer of that year when the world looked as if wanted to change direction and go to quite a different place from where it actually went), contains all the elements necessary for defining rock as a "genre" and as an "attitude."

Essentially, it's two chords joined by a bridge that never leads to a refrain and then ends with a dominant closing riff: a hypnotic sequential rhythm, without development, so the song is never the same length in any of the countless live versions that all the band, especially Lou Reed, performed later. As an "attitude," because if we're looking for total "rebellion," the destruction of rules, getting right out of a society that understood only mainstream, well, it certainly wasn't The Rolling Stones, or The Beatles, or Dylan who were laying down the law, but The Velvet Underground, hanging out in alleyways and in art galleries, poets of a rock that mingled with lowlife in just the same way it entered luxury apartments, rock that could be itself precisely because it was not bound by any framework. "I'm Waiting for the Man" is a story of life, yet again, and it hasn't aged one bit, because the theme (diversity, drug dependency, marginalization), sadly, is still current news that we are confronted with daily.

In any case, it could be said that "I'm Waiting for the Man" is a forerunner of "hard" rock, both in terms of sound and of content. Undoubtedly Lou Reed and John Cale's poetics at the time were a source of inspiration for a generation of musicians who had considered exiting from the glorious season of beat by electrifying their instruments and their hearts to give rock a more solid, tougher structure, at times granitic, and found the genre on solid ground. It's really difficult to say, in our context, how hard rock was born. There are so many versions, even if not contrasting. For the sake of simplicity, let's say that slipping out of one decade into another, especially on the '68 wave, rock decided that the color of flowers and the scent of incense weren't enough and that rock, having lost its innocence, should have been singing of other things, with rhythm and force totally different from those of the past. Even The Beatles had been aware of this, and with "Helter Skelter" they attempted to play "hard" and differently from the past. The Who caught on fast and decided to direct their sound towards decidedly more solid shores. Led Zeppelin saw it more clearly than anyone else, and stirred up their blues with increasingly edgy, electric riffs. The groups that arrived later completed the "revolution," transforming the sound into a genre: Black Sabbath and Deep Purple (each from their own standpoint) for the UK, MC5 and The Stooges in the United States. The latter, especially for their contribution of an irresistible figure like Iggy Pop, are among those who exercised most influence on the generations that followed, also because while hard rock may well have been a British brainchild in many ways, it was in America that it found fertile terrain to grown and develop, until it became, in more recent times, Heavy Metal.

While all this was happening, rock, in reality, was searching for other ways to renew its universe and, especially thanks to a small group of authors and musicians, sought to attribute new meanings to the world "spectacularity." Just ponder David Bowie, Roxy Music, and Marc Bolan of T-Rex, and you'll get quite an exact idea of what "glam rock" was: a style that had enormous driving and creative energy, in particular thanks to the artists we've mentioned. Its success was extravagant, bolstered by (decidedly less brilliant) groups and individuals like Slade or Gary Glitter.

▲ 2

▲ 1

1. Singer Iggy Pop, 1973.

2. Keith Emerson performing with Greg Lake, 1978.

3. A portrait of Brian Eno, 1974.

▲ 4

▲ 5

4. Robert Plant in concert, New York.

5. Rod Stewart performing, 1976.

In Italy we were able to understand the scope of the phenomenon when we saw home-grown girl Raffaella Carrà belting out "Rumore" or the debut of Renato Zero. Glam had some extraordinary peaks of creativity, especially in Bowie's work, up to the early Eighties, with a series of utterly legendary songs, not to mention Roxy Music, who mixed avant-garde, rock, glam, pop, and other stuff too, especially in their first two discs, aided and abetted by no less an accomplice than Brian Eno.

So here we are, in the UK at the end of the Seventies, when a new generation of bands arrived in that fateful year, 1977. The new arrivals have launched heavy criticism at their big brothers, considered prog rock little more than a fiction, an intellectualistic way of producing smoke without fire, thought that hippies and the leftovers were detrimental and ancient, and that millionaire rock stars had no interest in life, feelings, the emotions of the young, who saw no future ahead of them, and this was the really big problem.

In just a few weeks, from the explosion of The Sex Pistols and The Clash in the UK, of Patti Smith and The Ramones in the United States, the rock scene was turned upside down, record companies were pushed aside by independent labels, audiences deserted the old stars and the kids of the new generation took power with their ripped clothes, safety pins in their ears, and spiked haircuts in all manner of weird colors. Punk stole the limelight, burned like lightning and shattered everything that rock had become. Johnny Rotten's Sex Pistols turned the world of music on its head with a single album, but they were flanked by more enduring artists that included Patti Smith, Talking Heads, The Clash, The Ramones, The Buzzcocks, Joy Division, and each had their own sound, words to speak, that kids identified with.

If we think of a possible equation of maximum effect achieved with minimum effort in artistic communication, nothing in recent music history can be compared with the impact made on rock by the arrival of punk. First of all, it is wrong to consider it a musical movement, since that is imprecise and a contradiction in terms. It would be better to think of it as an action, a sign, a black scrawl scribbled on the image of rock, on hypocrisies and deviations, on distorted ambitions and decrepit clichés. All this happened in the second half of the Seventies and was once again on the usual transoceanic America-UK dialectics track. Where did the punk action begin? Yet again, history seems to be repeating itself. Certainly the roots can be found in America: groups like The Stooges and The New York Dolls had sown terror and jeering, harvesting at least the creation of a decisive band like The Ramones, and if the truth be told, their style had been perfected long before anyone had heard of The Sex Pistols.

The Ramones really are a case apart, four big obnoxious American kids who decided to take the helm of rock, and with hilarious cheek, back to its rock 'n' roll origins. They had a drop-dead formula: simple, direct guitar riffs, a fast, hammering beat, nasal, mocking voices, and various poses (see that of guitarist Johnny playing immobile, legs splayed, his guitar below his belly) that paved the way ahead. Curiously, considering that punk groups were at the very least blasphemous about the rock that had preceded them, we do know that the band pseudonym (each member of the band adopted the surname "Ramone," even though they were not related) was chosen as an ironic homage to the alias used by Paul McCartney for registering in American hotels.

So maybe America already spoke punk without knowing it, and basically the remotest forerunners, like Velvet Underground, MC5 and others, did come from the US, but again, the UK played its part to ensure the new movement took on a definitive, material shape and, above all, exploded into the music world in an event from which there was no going back. For the slap in the face to echo soundly and hit the mark as painfully as possible, it needed the masterly touch of a rascal like Malcolm McLaren, who successfully set up an improbable and ungovernable band named The Sex Pistols. The name communicated just how sharp the shock was going to be: there are occasions when a name carries or determines a fate. The fact is that the Sex Pistols really did shoot, an explosion that reeked of sex and unwholesome odors, stale beer and spit. It was just the one bullet, a decisive one, and the band called upon to fire it was a non-band, a gang of desperados with nothing to lose. Singer John Lydon changed his name to Johnny Rotten and the Russian roulette started. A couple of rough-and-ready badly-played songs, sung as if they were about to vomit, menacingly entitled "Anarchy in The UK" or "God Save The Queen" and the whole world noticed them. The Sex Pistols were the right thing at the right time, a flash-point, an sudden upheaval, a waft of ether up the noses of rock fans.

What remains to be understood is why one album and so little else produced by The Sex Pistols was, at the end of the day, so overwhelming. To understand this, we'll have to go back to those years, a dismal, menacing time when, for the first time, the oil crisis revealed the vulnerability of the Western system. Rock, for its part, was losing itself in complex labyrinths, seeking progressive ambitions, covering tortuous, fascinating, complicated routes, that were certainly drying out rock's chief source of energy: its immediacy. Revolt was in the air, shaking the new adolescents, who turned up their noses at the rock legends that were the legacy left by the previous generation. They wanted something of their own, something new, something wild; they didn't want to feed on the memories of their older brothers. Then the flames went up. However strange it might seem today, the phenomenon really did scare people. Record companies tripped over themselves to get rid of the band, radio banned their records, and all this did was increase the presumed integrity of the Sex Pistols in the eyes of their fans. But if the Sex Pistols burned out in just one season, with the tragic epilogue of Sid Vicious, punk sought less ephemeral expression, empowered in the voices of other groups. The Clash, for instance, also started off wanting to destroy everything. But when they got to the point of recording *London Calling*, they decided to redefine, rather than erase, what rock might be in those days.

In any case, an amazing number of groups flourished in America and, rightly or wrongly, were embraced by that compelling time, including more intellectual reflective musicians, with greater ambitions for their poetic mission like Patti Smith and Talking Heads, whose music flowed over into the New Wave that was happening in the UK.

Over and above the immediate uproar it caused, punk can be thanked for awakening consciences and at least forcing everyone to deal with the new world. Dark visions appeared on the scene, such as The Cure, who were somehow bastard offspring of punk, evokers of a blackness that darkened everything, canceling shades and allusions, negating colors, and consequently hope, easy optimism, the gilt conventions of rock. Groups emerged that could not be directly included in the punk scene, but evidently restarted from there, learning the lesson and assimilating the fundamental principles. Groups like The Jam and The Pretenders would never have existed without punk, or at the very least would have been quite different. Even Seattle grunge can be considered in this light. So there's pure punk, historically circumscribable, and then there is an attitude that never completely disappeared and, in the Nineties, resulted in an outright revival. Today there are groups that define themselves as "punk" in no uncertain terms, more often there are traces of punk everywhere, metabolized, portrayed, cultivated in various threads of rock, and even in the most radical hip-hop.

Exactly as had occurred years earlier for rock 'n' roll, a call that for purification, an assurance of recovered innocence, punk performed a similar function. In 1977, seemingly orchestrated by a symbolically prepared fate, Elvis Presley died: still young, yet flaccid and bloated. The year before, the greats of rock had convened on a stage for The Band's farewell concert (filmed by Martin Scorsese) and called *The Last Waltz*, somehow an indication of symbolic awareness. Since then, the term "punk" continues to mean an extreme limit, a moving boundary that shifts step by step, as the media gradually absorb and foil the powerful energy that rock really evoked, at least in several fundamental moments.

Since then, the term **PUNK** continues to mean an extreme limit, a moving boundary that shifts step by step, as the media gradually absorb and foil the powerful energy that rock really evoked, at least in several fundamental moments.

SID VICIOUS, 1978 ▶
The bass-player during the Sex Pistols
New Year's Eve concert.

THE RAMONES, 1977 ▼
Johnny and Joey Ramone, Los
Angeles.

THE CLASH, 1979 ▼
Joe Strummer, Clash guitarist and
singer on stage in 1979.

THE CURE ▶
Lead singer Robert Smith during a
concert.

1970

SIMON AND GARFUNKEL

Bridge Over Troubled Water

1971

THE ROLLING STONES

Sticky Fingers

1970

THE WHO

Who's next

1971

MARVIN GAYE

What's going on

1971

LED ZEPPELIN

Led Zeppelin IV (Fours Symbols)

1972

LOU REED

Transformer

1972

DAVID BOWIE

The Rise and Fall of Ziggy
Stardust and the Spiders From
Mars

1972

JETHRO TULL

Thick as a Brick

1973

PINK FLOYD

The dark side of the moon

1975

BOB DYLAN

Good on the track

1975

BRUCE SPRINGSTEEN

Burn to run

1975

GENESIS

The lamb lies down on Broadway

1977

KRAFTWERK

Trans-Europe Express

1977

DAVID BOWIE

"Heroes"

1977

SEX PISTOLS

Never mind the bollocks, here's
the Sex Pistols

1977

TALKING HEADS

Talking Heads: 77

1977

IGGY POP

Lust for life

1978

PATTI SMITH GROUP

Easter

1972

ROXY MUSIC

Roxy Music

1980

THE CLASH

London Calling

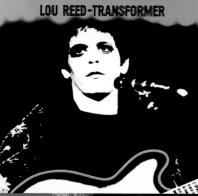

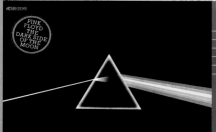

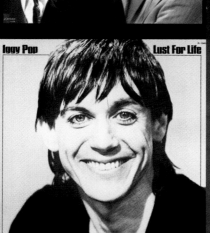

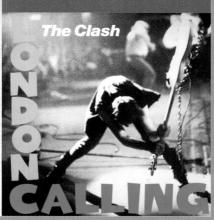

Bruce Springsteen Jackosn, Prince, Du Ballet, U2, Cure, S Gabriel, Elvis Costell Eno, Bob Marley, Paul Weller, Smith Kennedys, R.E.M., De

MICHAEL JACKSON
MICK JAGGER
POLICE
BONO
MICHAEL STIPE
MADONNA
PRINCE
BRUCE SPRINGSTEEN

Madonna, Michael
an Duran, Spandau
mple Minds, Peter
, Joe Jackson, Brian
olice, Dire Straits
New Order, Dead
a Soul, Public Enemy

80

Some think that, musically, the Eighties should be forgotten. Some only remember Duran Duran, hair metal, and Michael Jackson's video clips; others recall Ronald Reagan and Margaret Thatcher;

still others think of the exaggerated appearances, the religion of the superficial, fast, heavy drugs, the end of vinyl and the supreme rule of major record companies – the list could go on. All of that's true, no doubt about it, just as it's true that show business, which was in a fat cow period, tended to remember these things rather than others (ah, the inevitable Golden Eighties revival). Nor can the fact that there were other things that were decidedly better, more important, fascinating, singular, new and unique be overlooked. This was the first time since the Fifties that the universe of youth had sought to give itself a radically different musical slant, a clean break from the past, leaving rock behind. There was a split second when Eighties British rockers wouldn't dream of using the word "rock." In fact, the two words that preceded the word "rock" for defining the music of that period, in other words "New Wave," rapidly became more important than the term they were seeking to define. So what was "new wave rock" just became "New Wave," and the term rock fell quietly and discreetly by the wayside.

It wasn't an accident: punk stated quite clearly that music born in the Fifties had gradually, inexorably transformed either into commercial, industrial, or empty and repetitive product, that rock was reduced to a mere formula and that the entire youth culture universe had reached a point of no return. Once punk had obliterated the language of rock so thoroughly, it was going to be tough recovering anything to use as a basis for creating something new, because something new was undeniably required.

So an entire generation start moving and forgot, wiped out, refused the past and sought to recreate youth music with completely new ground rules. This turning point was also given a sound push in the right direction by the arrival of low-cost electronic keyboards, which made it possible to escape the stereotypical rock sound and enter a hypothetical futurist scenario, take a trip to the future without much cash in hand, using a sound-driven time machine that even responded perfectly to punk's required "zero level," which is to say simple, direct, essential sounds, no frills, no special effects, no solos, no personal prowess in the instrumental field. This was the basic ethos of New Wave: rock-free rock, negation of rock, which was establishing itself at the dawn of the decade, especially in the UK. If punk was still rock, goth, for instance was its next of kin, for its obstinate use of guitar, a predilection for long hair and a specific dress code, recovering only the melodic structure of music from the past, a preference for songs and, more deeply, love of darkness itself, which had been crucial to rock (Morrison, Hendrix and many others had flirted extensively with their dark sides and the dark side of music). The electronic new wave jeered, on the other hand, on a trail of seeking (or maybe even inventing) the Orient, preaching the end of rock in a radical manner and coming up with bands comprised of just digital keyboards and, in some cases, reducing music to pure "drum machine" beat, an icy, inhuman, sweatless electronic simulation of the good old drummer. Was this still rock? Of course. It was rock in the fullest sense of the word, precisely because it denied being a descendent of rock. Precisely because killing off the "father" defined its new unique nature, its new and

pristine language of youth culture. So it was rock, even if it didn't sound like rock, and actually really wanted, in some cases, to define a breaking point, the point of no return. Plenty of people said "Rock is dead" and in the end, the "death" of rock breathed life into a new rock, lacking the longwindedness of the many pretentious suites of late progressive, stripped of aspiring rock-star ambitions and once again linked to kids' lives, those of the new generations, whether Goths were expressing malaise or even desperation, trying to forge ahead on a journey into an inner "obscurity;" or electro-pop was announcing a decade of total non-commitment, lightness and vacuity. This was when Duran Duran and Spandau Ballet re-launched a "British invasion" of Ronald Reagan's America, abetted by the newly-arrived MTV.

This was the backdrop for the advent of U2 and Simple Minds, who began to lay down the rule of a new rock, appropriate for the times, using the latest technologies and applying the newest feelings. In the case of U2, above all, there was political and social commitment. In 1985, Live Aid was set up and the first "planetary" concert was performed, where rock, all of it and all together, got into gear to collect funds for the African famine-ravaged populations. The concerts were a great event that showed rock music continued to dream the same dreams, however much the sound might have changed.

Sixties rock was buried along with the dreams of the Sixties, and Seventies rock had been swept away by punk, which had exposed its fictions and myths. Guitars, primary symbol of an electric revolution, seemed old, useless instruments, only good for those who wanted to show technique in endless and equally robotic solos. Was there anything left to be done, then? How could anyone sing about a world that in such a short space of time had changed so deeply? Who would be listening, anyway? The punks, still hugging the limits of desperation? Junkies surviving the Seventies who had no clue where to go? Yuppies, social climbers, cynics, and hedonists who seemed to dominate the decade's generational scene? In the UK, the smarter personalities were keeping their distance for pure, simple rock, to mix it with infinite sensations, with totally different music and different atmospheres. Figures who had emerged with the New Wave, like Joe Jackson or Elvis Costello, as well as some of the greats of the previous decade: Robert Fripp, Peter Gabriel, David Bowie, and Brian Eno, pulled away from the traditional sound of rock and traveled towards new and often surprising shores. For the first part of the decade, the Americans failed to grasp what had happened to rock, and appeared stunned, confused. Anyone still convinced of the power of the guitar took refuge in metal, the noisiest, most potent effigy of rock energy. Anyone convinced of the power of the song, on the other hand, suffered the new wave, often enduring it and seeking to adapt, but most often failing to understand it.

Rock was born in the United States and this fact is historically undeniable. Nevertheless, it can't be denied that without the UK, The Beatles and The Stones, Liverpool beat and London rhythms, rock would definitely have been very different from what we now know and love. The debate on the "supremacy" of British rock or American rock is actually quite futile, because both sides of the Atlantic produced, sometimes at very different times and sometimes perfectly synchronized, top-notch musical material, fundamental works for understanding the nature and evolution of rock, and individual and memorable songs, without which, in a number of cases, youth culture itself would have headed off in a different direction. It makes more sense, however, to try and identify the differences between the two ways of composing rock songs, of "flirting" with pop, with melody, with the intention common to all periods of rock, of addressing not just the young, but all those who prefer the genre.

So, while in America it was pop that dominated, with Madonna and Michael Jackson, with pseudo-hard music imposed by MTV, like Mötley Crüe's heavy metal or Van Halen's melodic-electric rock, in the UK, an extraordinary generation of new singer-songwriters advanced. It is true that the Americans were capable of putting together two great types of music – country and blues – to create that unique and fertile terrain that assisted the growth and blossoming of rock 'n' roll, but it is equally true that the British were able to take the best of a decidedly different European musical tradition and sought to write songs in a different way, with more attention to structure, more refined in performance and with an eye to subcultures that American mainstream rock shared, but on a far narrower scale. Obviously not always, but for most of the Seventies, the songwriting scenario was at its best right in the United States, with figures of the caliber of Dylan, Paul Simon, Joni Mitchell, Neil Young, Bruce Springsteen, to name but a few of the most famous names, who have written some legendary, rock-solid music. However, the theme of this disc is the next phase, the Eighties and Nineties, a period when, after the virtual death of rock enacted by the punk scene, writing songs had become quite an enterprise and in America, in particular, "singer-songwriters" seemed to be suffering a time of real crisis (with the exception, of course, of individual artists who reached mass success precisely in that decade, like Springsteen, or cult figures like Tom Waits, to name just two). In the Eighties the law was laid down by British pop, with a handful of songwriters and figures who defined the boundaries of a style and promoted at home and abroad. The decade was significant because in the US the control of song gradually fell into the hands of black music authors, and in the Nineties and beyond, the sound and beat of black music dominated the stage.

There are few singer-songwriters today who can boast the intelligence, the history, or the creativity of Elvis Costello. In fact, calling him a "singer-songwriter" almost limits the description of his expressive abilities, because Costello is more than a singer-songwriter, he is a composer, a lyricist, a traveler in the world of sounds who tirelessly crosses frontiers and, when possible, tears them down. At the end of the day, it comes naturally to him to stand in the middle, suspended in that undefined musical territory that we still insist on calling "song," but which, in the hands of Costello, transforms into many different things. Since 1977, the era of his exciting debut album, *My Aim is True*, Costello has explored every possible popular music scenario, often drawing on highbrow music, flirting with film and stage, taking a detour into poetry, playing rock, pop, country, reggae, avant-garde and jazz, challenging himself endlessly, flanking Paul McCartney as easily as he did the Brodsky Quartet, without distinguishing one from the other very much, combined solely by his relentless passion for music.

Over the years, Costello's music (well, "musics") has been extensive and extremely varied, refined and cultured operations that were often followed by forays into the field of rock; experiments were set against a background of sheer enjoyment, because Costello, unlike his colleagues, has never fallen prey to market trends or temptations, and has continued, undaunted, along his way, even when a lot of his rock fans fell by the wayside, since he invariably found them waiting for him on the next leg.

Joe Jackson and Paul Weller were also children of the punk scene who survived subsequent decades, riding different waves; the former opted precisely for the music of historic American authors as a point of reference; the latter explored the creases of rock in a totally original way. They were flanked by figures who highlighted the extraordinary scope of rock song revival: Morrissey and Johnny Marr of The Smiths, a prominent band that combined exploration with popularity as few other groups of the time managed. The Housemartins, Fine Young Cannibals, even an ex-punk like Billy Idol, in the Eighties contributed to what was defined the "second British invasion" of the United States, bringing their sound to the attention of the whole world.

The New Wave produced just that, waves of new sounds that arrived not just from the USA and the UK. Germany, for instance, came to the limelight with many groups, including Einsturzende Neubauten and Nina Hagen's band; Italy managed to get in on the act with Litfiba; France came up with chart-toppers Telephone, witnesses to new European rock drive, a new generation of musicians who could offer new sounds and new sentiments.

The decade when ROCK died and was born again.

1. U2. An image of the Irish group, 1984.

2. Elvis Costello. The British singer, 1990.

3. Billy Idol. Concert in Rio de Janeiro, 1991.

1978

DEVO

Q: Are we not men? A: we are Devo!

1979

FRANK ZAPPA

Joe's Garage. Acts II e III

1980

THE CLASH

Sandinista!

1980

TALKING HEADS

Remain in light

1980

THE RAMONES

End of the century

1980

DEAD KENNEDYS

California Uber Allies

1981

TIN DRUM

Japan

1982

MICHAEL JACKSON

Thriller

1983

R.E.M.

Murmur

1983

THE POLICE

Synchronicity

1984

BRUCE SPRINGSTEEN

Born in the USA

1984

PRINCE AND THE REVOLUTION

Purple Rain

1986

PAUL SIMON

Graceland

1986

THE SMITHS

The Queen is dead

1987

U2

The Joshua Tree

1987

STEVE WINWOOD

Arc Of A Diver

1988

PUBLIC ENEMY

It takes a nation of millions to us back

1989

BONNIE RAITT

Nick of time

1989

DE LA SOUL

3 Feet hight and rising

1989

NEW ORDER

Technique

Red Hot Chili Pep
Jam, Soundgarden
Chemical Bros, Pi
Rage Against The
Smashing Pumpk
Pavement, Metallic
Williams, Green Da

KURT COBAIN
ANTHONY KIEDIS
CLIFF BURTON
BONO
BOB DYLAN
ROBBIE WILLIAMS
MADONNA

ers, Nirvana, Pearl
Oasis, Blur, R.E.M.
odigy, Sonic Youth
Machine, Radiohead
ns, Kaiser Chiefs
a, Coldplay, Robbie

90

We're at the point where we're in the habit of saying that yesterday's rock (but also the day before yesterday's) was better, much better, than today's.

We won't deny that in many ways that's true, even if just seen in the perspective of how long the period lasted: from the early Sixties to the mid-Eighties, when rock was the true language of the young generation, the main territory for creative experimentation, the preferred instrument of communication, for recognizing oneself and one another, for talking and listening. There was rock, and really there wasn't much else. Then when punk put paid to that rock, such as it was, there was an explosion of genres, sub genres, trends and, above all new sounds and new climates that knew how to interpret often faster, often better than rock, the dreams and needs of new generations. Rock, basically, wasn't dead, but had lost its centrality and had become one of the many languages that tribes of youth spoke fluently, one of the many tools that could be used when needed, at different times. A music ready to be reborn and die again, each time that a new generation appeared on the world horizon.

As far as quantity is concerned, it is certainly true that Seventies and Sixties rock was far richer than today. But for quality it's not quite so straightforward: it's more difficult, more involved. First of all, it's not easy to compare today's product with records that went down in the history of rock and contemporary popular music, like those recorded by the most famous artists of past decades, not least of all because today's artistic offering is unable to compete with a "historic" dimension, so we can't give it the same perspective enjoyed by the evergreens. We're not saying that a comparison of quality cannot be made: actually it's clear even now that no contemporary artist has released an album on a par with *Dark Side of The Moon*. At the same time, however, we should remember that a record like *Dark Side* became "historic" many years after it was released, just as we recall many albums today as having been essential in the development and evolution of rock history, that at the time of their recording, didn't obviously have this weight or this significance. We're saying this to underscore that even at a time when rock is just one voice of many heard in youth culture, thus losing some of its fundamental centrality, there has been no lack of composers, groups, solo artists, who have written and performed fantastic, important songs, many of which might not make it into the ideal rock history songbook in a few decades' time, but for today, they accurately illustrate our era, the current age, in all its confusion, passion, sound and sentiments.

In reality the sound of the new era wasn't one sound at all, but rather, many different sounds. New-era rock can't be one single rock, cannot offer the audience and the kids a single way of being or playing rock, but it does provide infinite and diverse opinions, many ways of interpreting and living the old rule. The great liturgical part of Sixties and Seventies rock is definitely over: today, each artist seeks their own approach without necessarily falling into the cliché of the concert performance, the spectacular exhibition of their own inventiveness. Certainly there are those who still do that, simply interpreting rock as a bunch of commonplaces, or even the quintessential "commonplace" of youth culture, with the "common place" obligatorily untouchable, unmoving, duly repetitive and, consequently, faithful to its roots, to its

nature. Nonetheless, most of today's rock artists aren't bound by a set rule and they perform their style freely, seeking to offer not "the rock," but "their own rock," their personal interpretation of the world. Each one proposes a different theory, but at the same time each artist establishes themselves through a strong sectorial choice, perhaps tougher, more important, and more determined than in the past: the sector of rock. What we're basically trying to say is that in the Sixties and Seventies it was easy, almost obvious, natural, to be a young person choosing rock as a personal means of expression, but today it's not so easy, spontaneous, or natural. Choosing rock really does mean "choosing," precisely because today there are far more languages available and they are all "legit" in the sphere of youth communication. Choosing rock means entering a zone of youth communication, in any case, which appears undoubtedly as more "adult," less consumerist, less light and fast than that linked to more direct, spontaneous, trendy languages, like rap and techno, just to mention two of the important cultural and musical phenomena around today.

1991

NIRVANA

Nevermind

1991

RED HOT CHILI PEPPERS

Blood sugar sex magik

1992

RAGE AGAINST THE MACHINE

Rage Against the Machine

1992

PAVEMENT

Slanted and Enchanted

1992

R.E.M.

Automatic for the people

1993

COUNTING CROWS

August and everything after

1994

OASIS

Definitely Maybe

1994

BLUR

Parklife

1994

SOUNDGARDEN

Superunknown

1995

SONIC YOUTH

Washing Machine

1995

BRUCE SPRINGSTEEN

The ghost of Tom Joad

1995

THE SMASHING PUMPKINS

Mellon Collie and the infinite sadness

1997

THE CHEMICAL BROTHERS

Dig Your Own Hole

1997

BOB DYLAN

Time out of mind

1997

RADIOHEAD

Ok computer

1997

PORTISHEAD

Portishead

1999

TOM WAITS

Mule Variations

1997

BUENA VISTA SOCIAL CLUB

Buena Vista Social Club

2005

KAISER CHIEFS

Employment

2005

SUFJAN STEVENS

Come on feel the Illinoise

1

3

1. Kurt Cobain. Nirvana take part in
   MTV Unplugged, New York, 1993.

2. Marilyn Manson in concert, 1999.

3. Axl Rose. Guns N' Roses at the
   Freddie Mercury Tribute Concert, 1992.

So what was Nineties ROCK and what is today's rock?

Difficult, really, to offer a good definition for everyone, because in the Nineties the American empire recaptured its power over rock, especially thanks to a bevy of Seattle bands, ready to invade the world with grunge, full of electric rock and rubbing shoulders with metal sounds, but unfettered by any collusion with the hard-rock image, without rules or constrictions, abounding with real passions to be expressed, ready to stage the Generation X screenplay that had disappeared from the press and TV, lived underground for a while and erupted on the wave of the music of Kurt Cobain's Nirvana. No different from the Sex Pistols or Hendrix epics, Nirvana's heroics lasted only a brief spell, with Cobain burning himself and his music out in a handful of years, but just long enough to change the actual perception of rock, which seemed faded and lost, but then made a dazzling comeback with Pearl Jam, Soundgarden, Mudhoney and many others, recapturing the feeling. In the UK the situation was different and new Brit pop was emerging: Oasis, Blur, then Radiohead, Pulp, Supergrass and dozens of other bands, each with its own sound, its own theory, none of which were sufficient to put a generalized version of rock back on the throne. Leading the way was rap, with its fast, direct language that transformed it into the rock of the new generations; there are the technologies, with computers ensuring every house has music. Rock is no longer in its focal role, it is just another of the various soundtracks to our lives, often the child of nostalgia, sometimes aspiring to express some novelty.

Today there isn't just one rock, but a multitude that meet and mingle, young languages that intersect and old sounds that tend not to vanish, but actually return with renewed energy.

Stars no longer have the rough look of bygone times: they are pop stars, like Robbie Williams, or rappers balanced between violence and good nature, like Eminem, and for both the rock universe is just a distant reference. A close look at rock today, as we perceived it in the twentieth century, has almost disappeared. But there is still fire under the embers, because rock, really, won't ever die. Each time it seems to vanish but rises out of its ashes, every time it is declared dead, someone revives it. Because each time, on the stage of life, a new generation arrives, grabs a guitar, plugs in an amplifier, powers up and strums life into dreams and ghosts that no one else can express.

ROBBIE WILLIAMS ▶
2006 concert, Mexico City.

OASIS ▶
Noel Gallagher sings at the
2007 BRIT Awards.

BLUR ▶
Graham Coxon, Dave Rowntree,
Alex James and Damon Albarn.

EMINEM ▶
MTV Awards, New York, 2000.

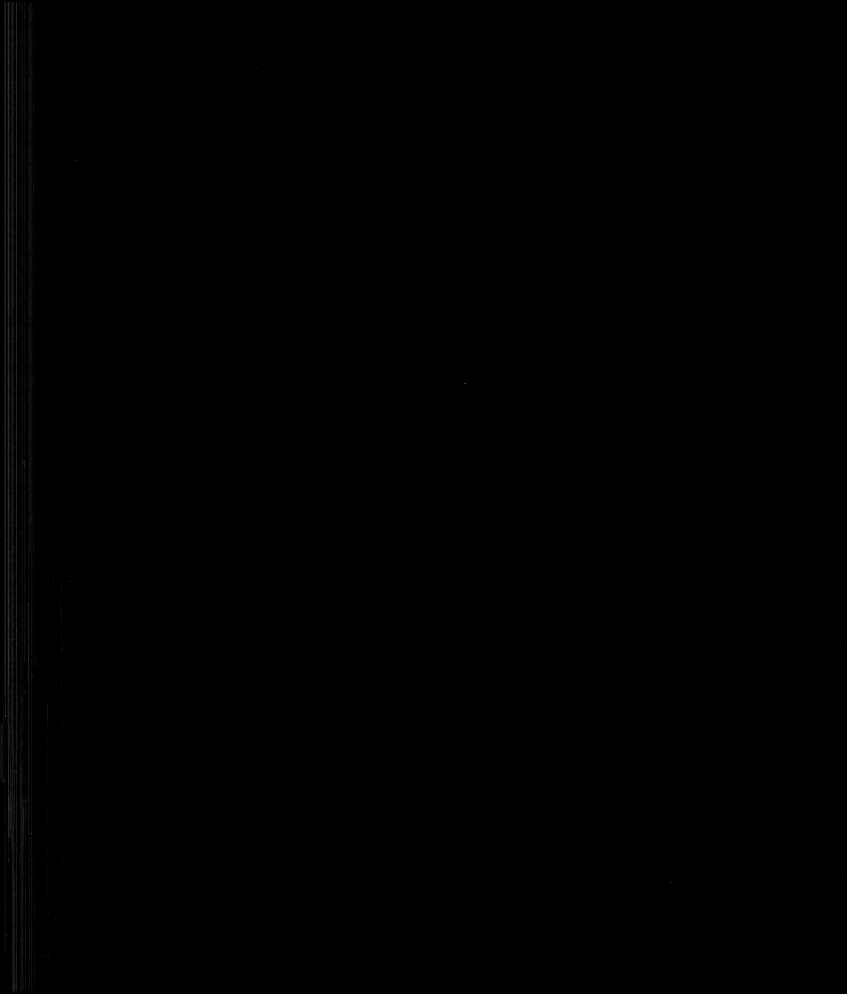

IT'S ONLY
ROCK'N'
ROLL
(BUT I LIKE IT)

Vernon Elvis Presley and Gladys Love Smith Presley brought up the future King of Rock 'n' Roll in Tupelo,

Mississippi, until he was 13, when they moved to Memphis, Tennessee. The 1949 move was to Lauderdale Courts, a

housing project in a working-class neighborhood where many other musicians lived. The neighborhood was also home

to Beale Street (where blues musicians hung out), Ellis Auditorium, and the Poplar Tunes record store. Sun Records

studios were just a mile away. Elvis began playing the guitar when he was only 11, but in Memphis he discovered music,

playing in the yards and dance halls at Lauderdale Courts as he finished high school and went to work as a truck driver.

In the summer of 1953 he paid four dollars to record the first of two dual-sided demo acetates at Sun Studios, which was

owned by Sam Phillips, the man who discovered Elvis. "My Happiness" and "That's When Your Heartaches Begin" were

popular ballads of the time (featuring two keywords that were to hallmark Presley's life: happiness and heartache. Elvis

said he intended to surprise his mother, and maybe that was true, but fate took a hand. Sam Phillips heard the demo and

in June 1954 invited Elvis to replace a singer on a single. That didn't work out, but Elvis met two musicians, Scotty Moore,

who played guitar, and Bill Black, who played bass. A few weeks later, as they were rehearsing "That's All Right Mama" in

THE HEART

the studio, Sam Phillips pressed the record button without telling Elvis, and the first single was born. It was handed right

OF MEMPHIS,

over to Memphis' WHBQ radio station, who made it a local success.

THE "KING"

OF ROCK'N'ROLL

Elvis Presley

67 [ELVIS PRESLEY IN THE FILM "LOVE ME TENDER"] ▲ The young singer made his cinema debut in 1956, in a film directed by Robert D. Webb.

68 [HOLLYWOOD, 1956] - Elvis on the "Ed Sullivan Show", 1956: the broadcast raised a storm and his popularity rocketed.

69 [CONCERT IN MEMPHIS, 1956] - Elvis's live performances were a huge success with teenagers, especially girls.

Elvis began playing in Tennessee, and with screaming girls hot on his heels, his fame spread like bushfire in the next few months. Over the next year, he recorded five singles and in 1956 he shocked America by grinding his hips while he sang, earning his nickname Elvis The Pelvis. It was so controversial that when he appeared on *The Ed Sullivan Show* in front of 50 million viewers, they filmed him only from the waist up. Elvis became the subject of sermons that pinpointed him as Satan in person.

For all the musicians who came later, from The Beatles onwards, he was a role model, whether they were aware of it or not. Before Elvis, pop culture didn't exist and after him pop culture became "Culture," period.

The phenomenon can be described in various ways. Record sales, for instance: from 1956 to 1962, Elvis Presley cut 24 singles that consecutively made the Top Five in the hit parade, each selling over a million copies, and 9 making the number one slot (only Madonna equaled that when she had 9 consecutive Top Five hits in the late Eighties). He had 38 hits in the *Billboard* (world's official record industry magazine) Top Ten. That record is unbeaten, with Madonna second with 35 and The Beatles third, with 34. Or we can look at it from a musical perspective: He was the first to try fusion, which he did precisely with his first single for Sun Records by mixing white country and black blues music: "That's All Right Mama"/"Blue Moon Of Kentucky" (Sun 209, issued 19 July 1954).

70-71 [ELVIS PRESLEY 1960s] - His success and his popularity continued to grow, earning him the nickname "The King".

73 [TAPING "THE 1968 COMEBACK"] - The production of a TV special marked Elvis's return to music and live performances.

The historic
"ROCK ERA"
ended with him
and gave way
to the current
"POP ERA."

Elvis Presley

74 [CONCERT IN FLORIDA, 1974] - Worn down by his health problems, he continued his US tour.

75 [PROVIDENCE CIVIC CENTER, RHODE ISLAND, 1977] - This was one of his last concerts: Elvis Presley died a few months later, on 6 August 1977.

Elvis Aaron Presley (8 January 1935 – 16 August 1977), King of Rock'n'Roll. Born in a one-room house in Tupelo, Mississippi, and died in a massive mansion called Graceland in Memphis, Tennessee. Elvis was an enigmatic figure: following his fall from grace in the Sixties due to the popularity of The Beatles and the Woodstock Generation, he made a comeback in the Seventies when The Beatles' popularity declined. He played fantastic concerts in Hawaii and in Las Vegas, becoming America's iconic figure, but he was also an artist who withdrew increasingly from the outside world, locked in his painful, glittering dream. He had been destroyed by drug abuse, and afraid of aging. The King of Rock'n'Roll died alone, killed by heart failure, aged 42, in his Graceland mansion. The period of history called the "Rock Era" died with him, and was followed by the "Pop Era," which still goes on. Many still weep for him, some report sightings of him. The Legend.

Dylan's first two albums, cut between 1961 (*Bob Dylan*) and 1963 (*The Freewheelin' Bob Dylan*),

were acoustically identical to 1992's *Good As I Been To You*. Thirty years later, the minstrel from Duluth,

Minnesota, seemed to be sending out a very clear message. While the entire world got busy with

celebrations of Dylan's 30 years in business, the electric poet was hiding behind a mask provided by the

great territory of American popular music, the mine Dylan had excavated as a kid and where he

obviously continued to dig, even when he became an adult, while inventing electric rock. We might well

consider this twilight gesture by the great father of rock as it seems to indicate a direction, or at least

hint at an invitation to reflect on what had been done and what it meant, from the early Sixties, when

A GUITAR,

he made the leap that had to be made, in other words creating from the ashes of American folk music,

A VOICE,

new modern folk, urban, electric folk, which eventually became modern rock.

A POET

Bob Dylan

77 [LOS ANGELES, 1986] ⏷ 1986 concert for Amnesty International – "Conspiracy of Hope", at the Los Angeles Forum.

78 [LONDON, 1965] - Bob Dylan on the set of his music video for "Subterranean Homesick Blues".

79 [1965 PORTRAIT] - In March 1965 "Bringing It All Back Home" was released; the album was a fusion of folk and electronic rock'n'roll.

80 [BOB DYLAN IN CONCERT, 1960s] - Guitar and harmonica were the only instruments backing Bob Dylan during his concerts.

81 [NASHVILLE, 1969] - 1969: Bob Dylan on the Johnny Cash Show for the American ABC network.

It is worth remembering that in 1961, when 20-year-old Dylan arrived in Greenwich Village, New York, from icy rural Minnesota (where he nevertheless acquired a musical initiation, participating actively in the underground scene of the Saint Paul university campus and the Dinkytown district), American music was split between the Elvis Presley phenomenon and traditional country music, while proletarian radical folk music like that played by Woody Guthrie was being heavily ignored by public tastes. Dylan's arrival in New York coincided with an unusual tumult among metropolitan student and artistic youth, so the breath of brusque social energy expressed by the classic protest songs Dylan chose, or by similar pieces he wrote himself, struck the imagination of the habitués of dedicated venues like Cafe Wha? or Gerdes' Folk City, forcing New York *Times* music critic Robert Shelton to mention this skinny, curly-mopped folksinger as someone who was definitely going places.

A few weeks later, in November 1961, John Hammond signed him to Columbia Records to cut his debut album; Dylan had only arrived in New York on January 24 of that year.

November seems to be Dylan's lucky month: on November 16, 1992, thanks to satellite TV, 500,000 people worldwide watched the great concert organized to celebrate his three decades in music at Madison Square Garden in New York, his real artistic home. Dylan shared the stage with George Harrison, Eric Clapton, Tom Petty, Johnny Winter, Kris Kristofferson, Neil Young, and many other old and new talents, all present to pay homage to the Great Old Man (at 51 years old) of rock music. They acknowledged Dylan as the architect of the greatest aesthetic revolution of the twentieth century and the creator of a supranational artistic language that successfully interpreted not only ideologies, but also racial, religious and cultural differences, and the truest emotions of the young for the previous 30 years, renewing as time passed because, as Dylan himself said: "The times they're a-changin'."

82 [CONCERT FOR BANGLADESH] - New York's Madison Square Garden, in 1971, Bob playing with George Harrison (left), Leon Russell and Ringo Starr in a concert for Bangladesh, torn by civil war.

82-83 [RUBIN "HURRICANE" CARTER] - A concert in support of the famous boxer unjustly accused of murder. Joni Mitchell, Joan Baez and Richie Havens also took the stage. Bob Dylan's 1975 "Hurricane" was dedicated to the boxer.

1. Bob Dylan's 1978 UK concert at Camberley, Surrey.

2. Bob Dylan in concert, Los Angeles, 1980s.

▲ 3

▲ 4

3. Dylan in the 1985 "Farm Aid" benefit, playing at Champaign, Illinois.

4. Bob Dylan on stage, 1988.

86 [2000 OSCAR AWARDS, LOS ANGELES] - Bob Dylan takes the Oscar for the song "Things Have Changed" from the film "Wonder Boys."

A brief overview of Bob Dylan's career is nearly impossible: there was his strong influence on the Sixties Pacifist Movement, when classics like "Blowin' In The Wind" and "A Hard Rain's Gonna Fall" became maxims for world youth. Then there was the musical revolution that the genius from Duluth stimulated with several historic albums like *Highway 61 Revisited* or *Blonde On Blonde*, where new folk songs combined with the best of contemporary rock trends, creating the fusion that from that moment became a classic and would open the door for musicians in every corner of the world.

Nonetheless, Dylan today, venerated as a maestro the world over, has retraced his thoughts back to his true teacher, and in volume one of his autobiography, *Chronicles*, Dylan pays homage to Woody Guthrie, the great folksinger who sang of social protest during the Great Depression and throughout the Thirties and Forties. Dylan went to New York to talk with Guthrie on his deathbed, and the great old man gave him a sort of blessing for the future. Which is still his — and our — present.

The world's music has not been the same since. Many still miss the quartet who made the Sixties "fabulous" for eight long years, until they split on April 17, 1970. According to the 1983 book *Rolling Stone's Encyclopedia of Rock*, The Beatles had an incalculable impact on Western culture. We could still agree with that brief statement. No group had had such a profound effect on Western music, inventing it as a cultural genre. If the advent of Elvis Presley in the late Fifties created an American cultural legend, and the arrival of Bob Dylan in 1961 created a radical, cultured hub of youth music, only The Beatles, from 1962 onward, gathered under their banner all world youth, creating a cultural and generational divide that never healed.

With the arrival of The Beatles a whole reference grid collapsed: youth education in the post-war period was still character-ized by educational theories that envisaged a sort of lengthy apprenticeship under the protective, reassuring, and severe family and school wing, both representing the highest authority: the State. The claims of a new category, youth, burst forth in various ways. There were the literary, theatrical, and artistic avant-gardes, and Elvis Presley was emerging in music. Only The Beatles and Bob Dylan (with The Rolling Stones hot on their heels), however, were strong enough to break down the solid, stereotyped mental structures.

ALL FOR ONE - FOUR OBEs AT THE COURT OF BRITISH POP

The Beatles

89 [THE BEATLES] ▲
From the left: John Lennon,
George Harrison, Paul McCartney
and Ringo Starr, in the 1960s.

90-91 [THE BEATLES IN "A HARD DAY'S NIGHT"] - The group running through a deserted London street, in a scene from the 1964 comedy "A Hard Day's Night."

91 [FANS IN DELIRIUM, 1965] - The police struggling to keep the group's fans in check outside Buckingham Palace, London. The Beatles were awarded OBEs by Queen Elizabeth II.

The world was never the same again. The avalanche that began continued to spread. It was no coincidence that a great youth awakening occurred in the Sixties. After years of suppressed energy and feeling cut off from decision-making process-es, young people jumped into the fray, unexpectedly finding themselves in the lime-light, proving that youth had something to say about a great many things. The mental awakening had vast consequences.

Two crucial years — 1967 in America, 1968 in Europe — were undisputed historical watersheds, after which our entire culture-our societies, traditions, and ideals- changed for good. How was it possible that all this came about because of a pop quartet? The whole thing would be unbelievable if it hadn't really happened. Obviously, it was not just the musi-cal aspect. As far as The Beatles are concerned, the musical plane should be separated from the social side. This is precisely the second — and symbolic — level where the trigger of their effect on the culture of millions of persons must be sought.

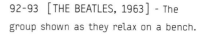

93 TOP [THE BEATLES 1960s] - A shot of the group that became a worldwide icon, used on badges and gadgets.

The Beatles were able to become the prodigious force of innovation they did become not because they were musicians but because they were symbols of transgression; examples of change.

However, apart from the magical name of the great phenomenon they became, The Beatles were also four Liverpool lads from lower middle-class families, keen to get out of their home city and driven by a dream blown in from afar; a dream that began in America and ended in the port of Liverpool. It brought innovations, trends, curiosities, and music, which found minds greedy for everything in those grey, difficult Fifties when Paul, George, Ringo and John were growing up. Years of deprivation in the aftermath of the war, years when England was licking her wounds from a war won with great effort, with great damage, which left a future to be totally reinvented.

94 [CONCERT, SHEA STADIUM, NEW YORK, 1965] - Mass delirium for the British group during their historic American concert. The performance, one of several in the US, consolidated their name in the States.

"Maybe in the Sixties we were naive. Everybody said, 'We didn't get a wonderful world of just flowers and peace and happy chocolate, and it won't be just pretty and beautiful all the time.' Just like babies, everyone went back to their rooms and sulked. 'We're just going to play rock and roll and not do anything else, because the world's a horrible place, because it didn't give us everything we cried for.' Right? Crying for it wasn't enough. The thing the Sixties did was show us the possibilities, and the responsibility we all had." The speaker was John Lennon in an interview he gave at Geffen Records' New York offices the morning of December 8, 1980, following the release of his *Double Fantasy* album. He went on to comment that in any case the Sixties had offered a ray of hope, but in the Seventies that went up in smoke, and in the Eighties it was time to plan the positive part of life. A few hours later, John Lennon was murdered. The interview became an unbelievable and involuntary testament. The same could be said of the entire Beatles story.

95 [CIRCUS-KRONE-BAU, MUNICH, 1966] - The Beatles playing during their European tour. Wherever the Liverpool Four went, they were mobbed by fans, proving how their success continued to grow.

[THE BEATLES BY ANDY WARHOL] - The British group in an image by artist Andy Warhol.

Is there anything else to be said about The Rolling Stones? For any rock critic or historian the band is a tricky

presence. For the last several decades — 1962 to the present day — The Rolling Stones have, for better or for worse,

occupied minutes or hours of our lives with their music, their presence in the news, their occult pressure as a mass

media phenomenon, as a lifestyle, as a behavioral model.

Musicians, artists, front-line proponents of the twentieth century's most popular music: rock, the only music that

could gather together billions of viewers in front of a screen at the same time (Live Aid 1985), or could attract three

and a half million people to stadiums to see the same band and hear the same songs (Stones 1989 USA tour), or bring

half a million people to the same place for three consecutive days (Woodstock 1969) – the Stones stood for all this and

more. They are a living heritage, the black culture's legacy to white culture. Through jazz and rock, now a universal

language understood by all four corners of the world, blues and gospel culture, the original culture of blacks

oppressed into slavery, survives. Rock carried a people's cry of pain and rock, simply thanks to this legacy, continues

to give forth a cry, at times stronger, at times weaker, for freedom.

MR. MICK JAGGER: SYMPATHY FOR THE DEVIL?

The Rolling Stones

99 [MICK JAGGER, LOS ANGELES, 1981] ▲ The leader of the Rolling Stones performs in a cloak made of two flags – the Stars and Stripes and the Union Jack. The Los Angeles concert was just one leg in the American tour that included several US cities.

100 [IRREVERENT PROMOTION] - The group poses for a promo shot for the famous "Have You Seen My Mother, Baby, Standing in the Shadow?", from the album "Between the Buttons," released in 1966.

101 [ROLLING STONES, GREEN PARK, LONDON] - The group caught as they stroll through London's Green Park. From left to right: Charlie Watts, Bill Wyman, Mick Jagger, Keith Richards and Brian Jones.

Time sped by for The Stones, cadenced by the anxiety of living without a care for the mechanisms applied by others. Based on the first glance cast their way on the evening of April 28, 1963, by Andrew Oldham and Eric Easton at the Crawdaddy Club in Richmond, The Rolling Stones their first recording contact with Decca the very next day. It was a gratifying time, but it was more than that — just a few years sufficed to make The Stones a point of reference for other kids, the ones on a collision course with institutions, especially their contentment with acquiescent and dominated morality, with the acceptance of conditioning right down to the intimacy of their most personal conduct.

104 [CONCERT, 1977] - Ron Wood, Mick Jagger and Keith Richard playing a 1977 concert. Mick Taylor had left the group during the 1975 American tour and was replaced by guitarist Ron Wood.

105 [LONDON, 1999] - Keith Richards, the band's guitarist, was a founder member of the Rolling Stones, with Mick Jagger and Brian Jones.

From the start The Stones wanted the free and personal right to choose, which was totally in tune with the legend that was on its way from the Deep South of the USA to the shores of Great Britain, and this was noted chiefly by American critics. The Stones were brought up with *Huckleberry Finn* and the blues, with Chuck Berry's ironic words and John Lee Hooker's painful lyrics, with Muddy Waters and Jimmy Reed classics. The band romantically — and extremely strong mindedly — embraced a vagabond concept that was more a way of being always on the road. It was chiefly a life philosophy, a refusal, and possibly a fate.

The Americans caught on fast, because The Rolling Stones represented the fantastic America of its artists, and as Europeans and as artists they replied to the Americans (part in jest and part seriously) with that image in which they saw themselves reflected. Because often, nothing is more real than a reality filtered by artistic expression. Because The Stones' America really did exist.

However, the society they were rejecting also existed. The police existed and so did the drug problem (which, we mustn't forget, is not just an individual issue but also a large-scale criminal business). There was also the problem of their being in the public eye and their now planetary scale as big rock stars, since big stars influence the masses.

106 [TORONTO, 2003] - The Rolling Stones during a Canadian event in support of SARS victims.

106-107 [RED-LIPPED MOUTH] - The stage set for the 1978 Rolling Stones tour was the huge red mouth, used as a backdrop.

108 AND 109 [MILAN, 2006] – Just three years after coming to Italy, The Rolling Stones were back at the Meazza Stadium in Milan for a one-off concert. Top, the stage and maxi screen set up in the football ground; right, a close-up of Mick Jagger.

The Stones were big stars as early as 1967, and precisely in that year the UK opted for determined repressive action against unorthodox juvenile behavior. The best method, psychologically speaking, in these cases, was to attack the symbols. Thus the arrest, trial, and prison sentences for Keith Richards, Mick Jagger and Brian Jones. The latter, at the time the real Stones' icon, was especially targeted, and the may well have started on the road to his early death at age 26, on July 3, 1969, in his home of Cotchford Farm near Hartfield. Certainly there were problems within the band because of it, accentuated by the fact that Brian Jones was denied an entry visa to America for the 1969 tour because of his issues with British justice, so he left the group on 8 June 1969: a few weeks later he was dead.

Years have passed, and the band continues to wander the world, playing the same "devil's music" that rang first across the Mississippi and then in London, changing the twentieth century en route.

They were the protagonists of a desolate journey between poetry and music, between Thirties Berlin and Pop Art New York, pessimists with regard to the future of urban culture and visionaries, pioneers of a decadence that no one could have imagined in the Sixties, and which was to show itself in full in the Seventies. Against a mournful black background, we see two almost hypnotic faces – Lou Reed's sad gaze and the vague, intelligent smile of John Cale (a pupil of Bernstein) – staring out from the cover of *Songs for 'Drella*. However, if we tilt the image slightly, we can see a third face: in a singularly gothic effect, a silvery silhouetted Andy Warhol appears, his eyes closed and his chin resting on his hand, as if in contemplation. All three return, united on one plane: the Master and his two Pupils.

To revive the glories of the era of Pop Art New York and Sixties experimentation, to succeed in reuniting two musicians who had bitterly parted ways, it took the violent shock of a death: that of Andy Warhol. It was a shock that served as a powerful stimulus even at a creative level. *Songs for 'Drella* is a themed album, a sort of opera about the life of Andy Warhol. It is also a rock manifesto, an art that by this time was fully aware of its expressive potential. There were just three instruments: the piano, the guitar, and the viola; and two voices, plus a huge dose of regret and sincere love. This was the album generated by the reuniting of the two leaders of The Velvet Underground.

AVANT-GARDE AND ADVENTURE IN THE SLUMS OF NEW YORK

The Velvet Underground & Lou Reed

Just before Christmas Day, 1988, Lou Reed and John Cale holed up in Sigma Sound's New York City recording studios with just three weeks to compose and record an opus co-commissioned by The Arts at St. Ann's and the Brooklyn Academy of Music. *Songs For 'Drella - A Fiction* was performed by Lou Reed and John Cale at St. Ann's Church for a very special audience. Bill Flanagan wrote for *Musician* that Andy Warhol's funeral took place late, on the afternoon of Sunday January 8, 1989, when the faithful grouped under the falling rain on the sidewalk outside St. Ann's, a lovely Gothic church in Brooklyn. At four o'clock they entered in an orderly fashion, sitting on hard wooden benches and in the choir. John Cale and Lou Reed sat in front of the altar and performed an hour-long elegy for electric guitar and keyboards. They sang and played 14 new songs about the life of The Velvet Underground's old mentor while a slide show of Warhol paintings ran in the background.

From the magical season of 1967, when the legendary *Velvet Underground & Nico* was released (with the cover showing Andy Warhol's *Banana*, authentic serial Pop Art) to the present day, Lou Reed has crossed many boundaries: from drug abuse to the most diverse types of music (*Rock 'n' Roll Animal* couldn't be more different from *Street Hassle* or *Metal Machine Music*), he redefined the very notion of rock. He worked with Bowie and Dylan, but he never forgot who initially transformed him from a potential New York junkie into a pop superstar, simply by believing in his talent. Cale, bearer of absurd sounds (a tuneless electric viola, for example) for rock of that time, and Nico, queen of a Europe seen with suspicion (a German star of Fellini's *La Dolce Vita*, and girlfriend of Rolling Stone Brian Jones), made up the backdrop to Reed's descriptive frenzy, which also owed much to New York poet Delmore Schwartz.

111 [LOU REED IN CONCERT, 1970] ▲ The guitarist and rock vocalist Lou Reed left The Velvet Underground in 1970 to start a solo career with his "Lou Reed" album.

113 [THE VELVET UNDERGROUND, LATE 1960s] - The cult band of the New York music scene was founded by Lou Reed and John Cale, later joined by Sterling Morrison on guitar and Maureen Tucker on drums.

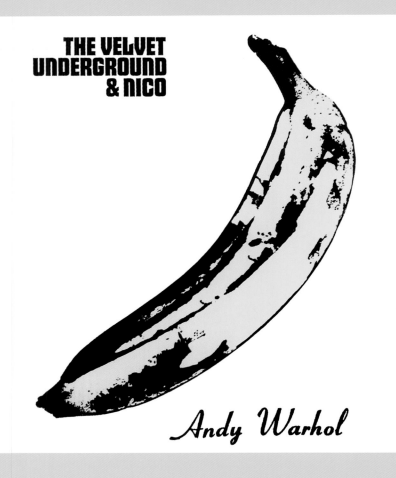

114 [THE VELVET UNDERGROUND & NICO] - The album was designed by the band's new backer: Andy Warhol. The original editions of the LP had a peelable banana, with the peel made from adhesive film.

114-115 [THE VELVET UNDERGROUND AND ANDY WARHOL, 1965] - Andy Warhol's arrival as producer totally overturned the group's music. From the left: Nico, German vocalist introduced to the band by artist Andy Warhol, Maureen Tucker, Lou Reed, Sterling Morrison and John Cale.

"My goal is to be one with the music. I just dedicate my whole life to this art." Perhaps Jimi Hendrix was aware that he was nearing the end when he made this declaration. It was 1970, and just a few months later his lifeless body would be found in a London hotel room. Jimi Hendrix died on September 18, the day after his performance at the Isle of Wight rock festival, the last time his musical genius appeared on stage. It was the end of a lightning musical career that lasted a mere three years as a soloist. Hendrix died alone and desperate for what he saw as the impossibility of having free rein with his immense talent. The breakup of The Experience and the bands that followed and his brief but meaningful friendship with Miles Davis and other music greats overwhelmed Hendrix and led to an increase in his already heavy consumption of drugs. Although the quest for musical creativity came with a price, for Hendrix there were positive aspects: "You have to forget about what other people say, when you're supposed to die, or when you're supposed to be loving. You have to forget about all these things. You have to go on and be crazy. Craziness is like heaven."

AN ELECTRIC GUITAR FOR INVENTING A MUSICAL RAINBOW

Jimi Hendrix

117 [JIMI HENDRIX, 1967] ⏶ The Jimi Hendrix Experience band took part in the Monterey Pop Festival, which was filmed by director D.A. Pennebaker for the film "Pop in Monterey" – the concert in which Hendrix burned his guitar.

118 [THE JIMI HENDRIX EXPERIENCE, 1967] - The group was founded in the UK, in 1967, with the line-up: Mitch Mitchell (drums), Jimi Hendrix (voice and guitar) and Noel Redding (electric bass).

119 [NEW YORK, 1968] - The Jimi Hendrix Experience at a New York press conference. The band's fame, just a year from its debut, was on a huge upswing, mainly thanks to Hendrix's performances, and his undisputed virtuoso guitar playing.

The musical development of this guitarist, born in Seattle, Washington on November 27, 1942, also touched a Dylan piece: "All Along The Watchtower," recorded by Hendrix in 1968 and part of the double album *Electric Ladyland*, this African-American's most complex and mature work.

The start of his rise to fame was "Hey Joe," a cover of the Billy Roberts classic recorded in 1966, which was a huge success as a single and the first that brought the name of Hendrix to the attention of the world. "Purple Haze," a metaphor for the psychedelic cloud, recorded by Hendrix in 1967, also confirmed his rock stardom, but his consecration as a true rock icon was his performance at the Monterey festival in California, during the summer of 1967. The festival glorified the new rock scene that was expressed by San Francisco's American counterculture: Hendrix, Jefferson Airplane, Janis Joplin, The Byrds – all symbols of America's new pacifist culture, that opposed the war in Vietnam and fought for civil and minority rights. At Monterey, Hendrix made a sensational gesture. In a highly symbolic ritual when he ended his set, he knelt down in front of his guitar, poured gasoline over it, and set it alight. It was a ceremony that caught the imagination of the entire rock nation.

121 [JIMI HENDRIX, 1960s] - Hendrix's favorite electric guitar was indubitably the Fender Stratocaster.

122-123 [HARLEM, 1969] - Jimi Hendrix during one of his last performances, in New York.

"The time I burned my guitar, it was like a sacrifice. You sacrifice the things you love. I love my guitar."

Hendrix wrote songs that also struck the listeners of the time: visionary, quite lyrical, very psychedelic. This is how he described them: "Imagination is the key to my lyrics. The rest is painted with a little science fiction." The music from the three albums he recorded during his lifetime, *Are You Experienced, Axis: Bold As Love,* and *Electric Ladyland,* fascinates millions of listeners. It is experimental music that explores the confines of rock as it was at the time. Featuring innovative use of the guitar as a sort of generator of cosmic sounds, the music sought all that was at the center of the universe, according to the Indian philosophies so in vogue in those days. Jimi Hendrix's Fender Stratocaster turned into a sort of universal antenna, a lightening rod of sound and noise deriving from a primordial creative nucleus. When Hendrix sang "Voodoo Child," he was declaring his spiritual autobiography in verse: a voodoo child, on an eagle's wing, taken to the outskirts of infinity. The lyrics are accompanied by the most powerful and metallic blues composed up to that time. Hendrix joined the Olympus of the greatest performers of his time and the passing of his genius is still a regret for many.

"THE TIME
I BURNED
MY GUITAR,
IT WAS LIKE
A SACRIFICE.

YOU SACRIFICE
THE THINGS YOU LOVE.
I LOVE
MY GUITAR."

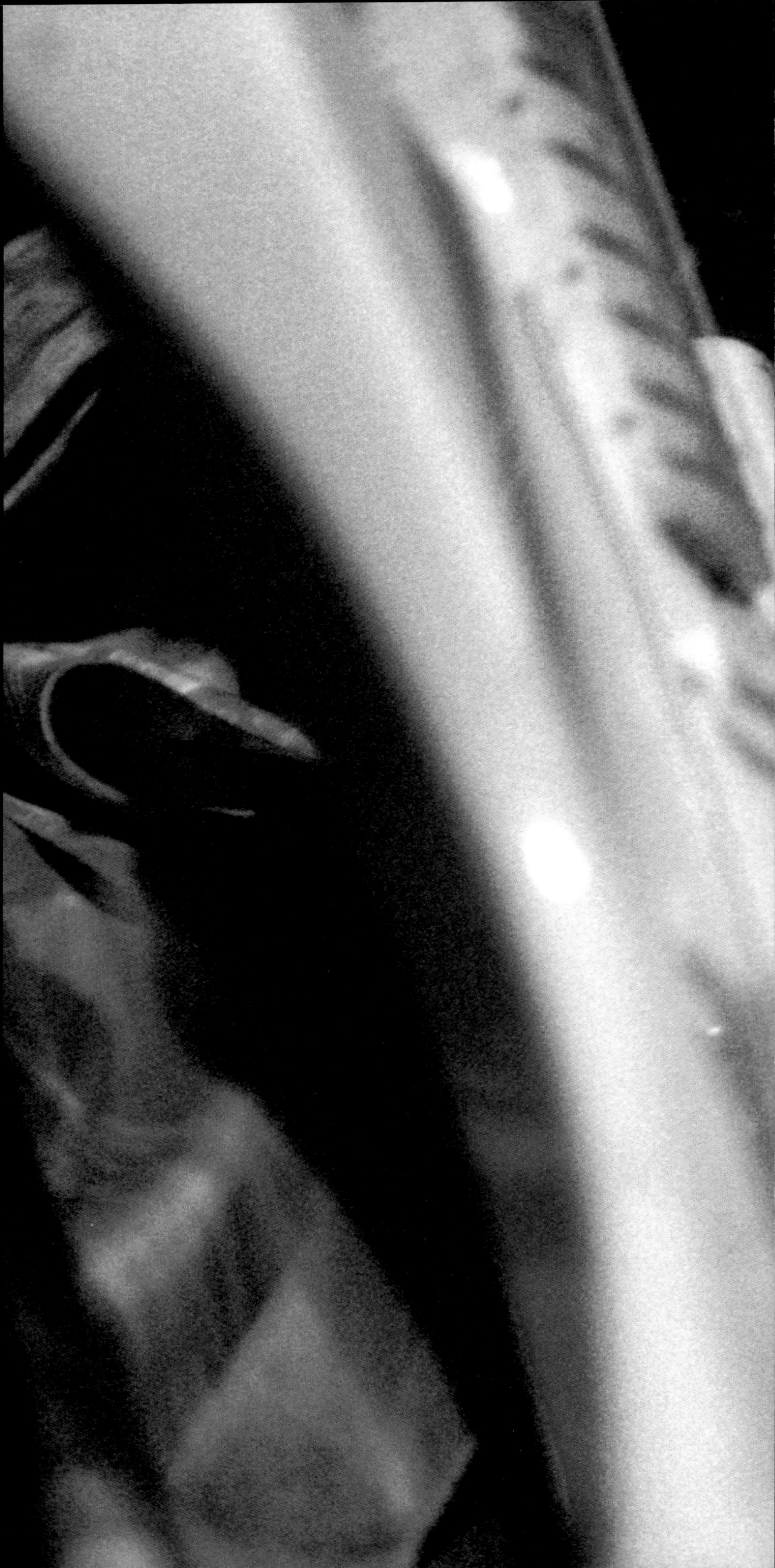

Jim Morrison (1943-1971) believed that words brought freedom, that poetry "opened all the doors." The Doors vocalist might have been born in the wrong place and time: he'd have been better suited, existentially, to Twenties or Thirties Europe. He'd have created poetry that liberated and transformed. He'd have been able to interact with philosophers and poets, playwrights and authors, actors. He'd have made films, his first love. He'd have been able to grow older than his 27 years, mature, turn into a Poet. In the Sixties, he was out of time. He was late but he was also ahead of his time. He was misunderstood by his compatriots, and admired by the rest of the world. This experience of exile and living death seems be a common fate of poets and philosophers, such as Nietzsche, Byron, and Pound. Morrison was a singer in a rock 'n' roll band, but he didn't feel that to be his true role. Morrison wrote something every day, otherwise it would have been a day lost.

The prologue to the book *Wilderness* (*The Lost Writings of Jim Morrison*), published in America by Villard Books, consists of a self-interview of Jim Morrison, in which he describes his relationship with poetry and writing. It is a truly illuminating text. "I'm kind of hooked on the game of art and literature; my heroes are artists and writers." Rock 'n' roll, like an audio Disneyland, was not literature, it failed to understand his poems, judged him, rejected him. Rock wanted spectacle, obscenity, bravado from him, and Morrison realized too late that he was trapped. His trip to Paris was just a last-ditch attempt to escape.

ROCK OPENS THE DOOR TO AWARENESS

The Doors

1246
MORRISON
HOTEL

125 [MORRISON HOTEL, 1970]
▲ The group poses at the
entrance to the Morrison Hotel
in Los Angeles, to promote the
album of that name.

126-127 [THE DOORS] -
The group was born, artistically,
in 1965 in Los Angeles,
California. The line-up was (from
the left) John Densmore (drums),
Robby Krieger (guitar), Ray
Manzarek (organ and keyboards)
and Jim Morrison (vocalist).

129 [CONCERT, 1968] - The band took its name from a William Blake quotation: "If the doors of perception were cleansed, everything would appear to man as it truly is, infinite."

It's tough for us to understand and difficult to separate the two personalities. The Poet and the Musician: one, the man (who reveals himself in his poetry); the other, the personality (born on stage and then tipped into reality). It's very difficult to differentiate between Morrison-author and Morrison-man.

In the summer of 1965, when he was reciting some of his writing to his classmate, Ray Manzarek, and he decided to initiate The Doors' adventure, he was surely another person. He was 22 years old, surrounded by a rapidly expanding culture, with drugs and sex as the horizon for initiating his self-discovery. The totality described by visionary poets, above all William Blake, nourished his soul. Six years later, he was stunned, depressed, maybe defeated, and found dead of a heart attack in a Paris hotel bathroom. More than anything else it was his long ordeal with American justice, in the Miami courts and especially Judge Murray Goodman, who issued the heaviest sentence for his acts of March 1969 (the charge was obscene behavior on a Miami stage), that left him shocked and distressed. Everything was in doubt: the music, the band, his very life.

The Doors had had their first taste of repression at the end of 1966, after a four-month Los Angeles contract as a house band for Whisky-A-Go-Go: after the first rendition of "The End" they were booted out of the club, because the lyrics were too explicit and with a sexual content. Their fate was sealed.

Morrison's legal scandals caused a huge uproar in America, despite them occurring in a period (the late Sixties) that was overwhelmed with other crucial events. The echo of those episodes, with exactly the same impact as those involving The Stones and their drug use in puritanical 1967 UK (Morrison encountered the same Puritanism, which crushed him), continued to spread for many years afterwards, attaching itself to the deteriorating image that Morrison had offered of himself, his life, and his work. Even after his death, the same prejudices and censures continued to emerge.

[JIM MORRISON, 1968] - The Doors' vocalist during a photo shoot for Life Magazine.

The Beach Boys were the Californian dream that the whole world shared. The titles of their successes, "Good Vibrations," "Surfin' USA," "Fun Fun Fun," "California Girl," and "Barbara Ann," as well as the easygoing surf melodies, vocal harmonies, and general musical cheeriness, all testify to the early-Sixties explosion of life, light, and music. In America, The Beach Boys were equal to or greater than The Beatles, witnesses to underlying innocence that was never permanently lost, but always recovered generation after generation. On the surface, they seemed quite ordinary, but they were actually extraordinary and not part of any category. They were light years away from New York and from the rules. In a Californian paradise, at the heart of the American Dream: the West Coast, where American territory slips into the ocean, but continues to expand in the minds of its inhabitants. In 1966, *Pet Sounds* interrupted the deep sleep the music had been in and resounded worldwide, touching on every musical and cultural register and ensuring a leap ahead for all pop music. It was experimental, light-hearted, and cheery, yet tragic at the same time. The Beach Boys became symbols of a youth seeking certainties, but full of desperation.

At the end of the Fifties, brothers Carl, Brian, and Dennis Wilson, their cousin, Mike Love, and their friend Al Jardine, all from Hawthorne, California, began making music and singing at friends' parties and on the beach, almost as a game. Al Jardine was originally interested in folk music, with serious lyrics, but at Dennis Wilson's urging, they sang about surfing, and the lifestyle that surrounded it. They were originally called The Pendletons, after the surf shirt that was so trendy at the time, but their name was decided when they

THE WILSONS:

recorded "Surfin'" in 1961. It got them noticed, and when their next single "Surfin' Safari" was released in June 1962, America raved

CALIFORNIA, SURF,

about them. It was as if the country had been waiting for them, as if they had invented the perfect soundtrack for John Kennedy's New

GIRLS AND SHEER

Frontier. After all, he was one of them – he just came from the other Coast.

BRILLIANCE

The Beach Boys

133 [THE BEACH BOYS] ▲ The group comprised the three Wilson brothers (Brian, Carl and Dennis), their cousin Mike Love, with friend and neighbor, Alan Jardine.

134 [CALIFORNIA, 1963] - The Beach Boys made their debut in the early 1960s, in California, at Los Angeles Long Beach Auditorium. "Pet Sounds" is considered one of the band's best albums.

135 [CALIFORNIAN BEACHES] - The Beach Boys are considered by most people to be the quintessential pop/rock combination group, synonymous with summer and Californian beach life.

Their first public concert was at the Ritchie Valens Memorial Concert on December 31, 1961, at the Long Beach Auditorium. Nearly two years earlier, on February 2, 1959, Ritchie Valens, along with Buddy Holly and the Big Bopper, had died in a plane crash. One could say that The Beach Boys carried on the spiritual legacy of these Fifties rock 'n' roll greats. Just like Valens and Holly before them, they helped create a whole new kind of music: they invented the "California Sound" and paved the way for other California bands like The Byrds, The Mamas and Papas, and Crosby, Stills, Nash & Young; they were their own producers — not even The Beatles had managed that; and they invented the concept album. In short, they were geniuses.

From the Seventies to the Eighties the Beach Boys were always strong enough to survive in a music scene that often seemed to forget their existence. In 1981, the compilation *Ten Years Of Harmony* signified the end of an era, but opened another door to more concerts and success. Today the album seems to be a final testament; in fact, just two years later, Dennis Wilson drowned at 39 years of age, off Marina Del Rey, California. Carl Wilson's death from lung cancer in 1998 and Brian Wilson and Al Jardine's pursuit of solo careers seems proof that despite their efforts at "Keeping the Summer Alive" (a 1979 single of theirs), for The Beach

A US pop and folk music duo comprised of Paul Simon and Arthur "Art" Garfunkel, they were amongst the most famous artists of the Sixties and several of their songs ("The Sound of Silence," "The Boxer," "Mrs. Robinson," and "Bridge Over Troubled Waters") became outright all-time easy-listening classics. They have won countless Grammy awards and are part of the Rock and Roll Hall of Fame. Their *Greatest Hits* album, an anthology of their Sixties work, is one of pop's best-selling records. In 1956, Paul Simon and Art Garfunkel met at Forest Hills High School, New York. They began playing together in a band called "Tom and Jerry" (yes, like the famous cartoon), with stage names of Jerry Landis (Simon) and Tom Graph (Garfunkel). In 1957 they started to write their own songs in the style of the Everly Brothers. They managed to record their first song, "Hey, Schoolgirl," for Sid Prosen on the Big Records label. The single was released both as a 45 and a 78 (the flipside was "Dancin' Wild"), and sold 100,000 copies, reaching number 49 in the *Billboard* charts. Later that year they played their song on *American Bandstand*, performing after Jerry Lee Lewis sang "Great Balls of Fire." In 1958 they tried to repeat the success of the single but failed, and after they left school, they went to separate colleges: Simon went to Queens College, New York, and Garfunkel to Columbia University.

WHEN SONGS BECOME POETRY

Simon & Garfunkel

137 [SIMON & GARFUNKEL, 1960s] ▲ Paul Simon and Art Garfunkel during a concert. Both musicians were from Queens, one of New York's five boroughs, and when they first began performing, in 1957, they went under the name of Tom and Jerry.

138 [SIMON & GARFUNKEL, 1967] - The duo posing for a promo photo shoot in 1967.

In 1963, the duo had reformed as Simon and Garfunkel and were involved with the Greenwich Village folk scene, playing with Bob Dylan. Simon asked Garfunkel to listen to a few of his folk songs: "Sparrow," "Bleecker Street," and "He Was My Brother," which was dedicated to Andrew Goodman, one of the three civil rights activists assassinated at Neshoba County on June 21, 1964. Goodman had been a friend of the duo and Simon's classmate at Queens College. In 1967, Simon and Garfunkel wrote the soundtrack for the movie The Graduate (directed by Mike Nichols and including the ultra-famous single "Mrs. Robinson"); the album was a record-breaker and in 1969, Simon won the Grammy for best original score. In March 1968, Bookends was released, which also went straight to the top ten. With this album the duo were finally rooted in the affections of the young community, with lyrics that began to define the new frontiers of pop music, the unease of a generation in the balance, the weaknesses and difficulties of living in a transition period. The album contained a fill version of the single "Mrs. Robinson" and this time it leapt to the number one spot on the charts and won the 1969 Grammy. Bookends also contained the famous "America" (a song of which Yes and David Bowie both did covers).

139 [PARIS] - Thanks to the success of "The Concert In Central Park," Simon and Garfunkel, who had split up several times and pursued successful solo careers, got back together for the 1992 world tour.

In 1969, Garfunkel began his acting career. Simon became frustrated with his colleague's numerous commitments and relations between the two deteriorated. The final tour concerts, in 1969, included famous performances in Carbondale, Illinois on November 8, and at Miami University in Oxford, Ohio, on November 11.

Although they have never officially got back together, Simon and Garfunkel have occasionally played concerts: the first time was at a Madison Square Garden concert in support of 1972 presidential candidate George McGovern. They also appeared on the October 18, 1975 episode of NBC's *Saturday Night Live*, playing "The Boxer" and "Scarborough Fair." They also a single "My Little Town" in 1975, which became a top-ten single (it was also included on both of their solo albums). Another famous episode was the marvelous concert in Central Park on September 19, 1981, which was the basis of what is probably their best-known album, *Live in Central Park*. Following the enormous success of this record, Simon and Garfunkel went on another concert tour.

Not only are they musicians who have been on the road for a long time, traveling companions of Dylan, witnesses of a bygone peri-

Led Zeppelin means, mainly, Jimmy Page, because of the profound fusion that exists between the guitarist's musical inspiration and the band's overall production. It is quite acceptable to say that Led Zeppelin was a being created and kept alive by the powerful musical fantasy of this reserved, snobbish, and shy man. Jimmy Page is man who looks fragile at first glance, a million miles away from the classic cliché of the outlaw-style rock musician – a stereotype shrewdly kept alive for marketing purposes.

Jimmy Page, looking more like an art student than a street kid with his slight build and poor, precarious health, was difficult to imagine getting to grips with the role of high priest for the mass rites that he later celebrated as part of Led Zeppelin. It was a role that Page enacted almost with detachment, without tumbling into the pathetic exhibitionism that affected many a rock star. Precisely because of the huge increase in the record market following the success of The Beatles, a large number of similar bands appeared in the UK, expecting to ride the crest of the commercial wave.

This was counterbalanced by a category of musicians who looked to America for inspiration and had no intention of writing commercial songs. These purists were committed to the blues, starting a revival of the genre, which soon acquired indigenous characteristics (British Blues).

THE CHAMPIONS OF HARD ROCK GO LOOKING FOR SOME HEAVY METAL

Led Zeppelin

141 [JIMMY PAGE, 1975] ▲ The famous guitarist was a founder member of Led Zeppelin and also their record producer.

142-143 [LED ZEPPELIN, 1970s] - An image of the group backstage, before a concert: Jimmy Page in the foreground, is drinking from a bottle of Jack Daniels. On the far left, vocalist Robert Plant.

143 [SYDNEY, 1972] - The British group performed in Australia and New Zealand, a 1972. That same year Led Zeppelin also toured the USA, Japan, Europe and the UK.

This hothouse of talent nurtured such bands as The Yardbirds. The band was starting to ride the new wave of rock success, which was linked to American counterculture, a mixture of psychedelia and hippyish oriental mysticism. Eric Clapton, the guitarist for The Yardbirds, soon left the band to its fate, unhappy with the commercial direction it was pursuing. He was replaced by Jeff Beck, a friend Jimmy Page's, and Page joined the band first as its bass player in 1966, then switched to twin lead guitar (with Beck). When two other members of the band left in 1968, Page decided to start a new band.

Thus Led Zeppelin was born. They were originally influenced by the phenomena of new psychedelic and oriental trends that The Beatles also contributed to mobilizing after they came back from their trip to India, but they soon broke away from both the political and the commercial currents, heading down their own musical path, which was unlike any other before or since.

Right from start, under the shrewd guidance of manager Peter Grant, Led Zeppelin's image was one of a band surrounded with an aura of secrecy and mystery, even keeping the band from TV and the press. In fact, Led Zeppelin was the only band that refused to appear in television programs (except one or two American megashows), never released (with just a few exceptions) promotional 45s. This attitude was in keeping with what was being preached at the time by youth counterculture movements (especially the hippies). Between 1968 to 1970, they became world stars.

144 [USA, 1970s] - Robert Plant and Jimmy Page on stage during an American concert.

145 [ROBERT PLANT, 1975] - Led Zeppelin's vocalist performing in an American concert. He stayed with band until 1980, when they split up following the death of drummer John Bonham.

Reaching the peak with "Stairway To Heaven," their songs had roots in Celtic and British folk music and J.R.R. Tolkien's books, which both Jimmy Page and Robert Plant, the band's provocative singer, were rediscovering at that time.

Page and Plant began writing "Stairway to Heaven" during their months in seclusion at Bron-Yr-Aur, a cottage in Wales. It was included on their fourth studio album, which was recorded in Hampshire, at the Headley Grange residence, between January and February 1971, using The Rolling Stones' mobile studio. Page remembers the December 1970 period as a time when Led Zeppelin put together a lot of new material in the Island Studios, but later moved to Headley Grange to try it out. Then they rented the mobile studio belonging to The Stones, having it delivered to where they were staying, a familiar place where the band was comfortable. This way there was a studio available and as soon as a good idea came up, the band could record it immediately..

"Stairway To Heaven" was played in public for the first time on March 5, 1971, at Belfast's Ulster Hall. Since then, and until 1980, when Led Zeppelin disbanded following the death of drummer John Bonham, the group wrote many memorable pages of classic rock, consecrated by the double live album and the movie *The Song Remains The Same*, filmed over three nights at Madison Square Garden, New York in 1973.

146 AND 147 [JIMMY PAGE IN CONCERT] - Jimmy Page's musical language during live performances was based mainly on the interaction between a Gibson Les Paul and a Marshall amplifier. A unique use of distortion, slide and acoustic guitars were what made the band's style so unusual.

148-149 [LOS ANGELES, 1993] - Jimmy Page performing with David Coverdale (vocalist of Deep Purple) in a 1993 concert, in California. That year the two musicians also produced an LP: Coverdale/Page.

Eric Clapton (1945–) began his career as a guitarist, first with The Yardbirds, a leading band in Swinging London,

then joining John Mayall's The Bluesbreakers, a real hotbed of blues talent (including Mick Fleetwood and Mick Taylor).

After a debut record of the same name with Mayall's band, young Eric formed a trio with bass player Jack Bruce and

drummer Ginger Baker. It was 1966 when Cream was born, bringing Clapton his first international success, which was

not overshadowed even when rock-music legend Jimi Hendrix, arrived in London to form the Experience, using the

Cream trio as a model. Eric Clapton's fame brought him the first of his nicknames, expressing in no uncertain terms the

devotion of his fans, because it was not rare at that time to read "Clapton is God" graffiti on London walls — simply due

to his skill in playing a Fender. His common sobriquet was "Slowhand," to describe his famously intense but controlled,

lyrical virtuoso electric guitar solos. Cream was a trio of virtuosos (Baker and Bruce were famed London jazz players)

that was able to improvise and play rock with a jazz attitude, shattering the barriers set up by Beatles-type pop songs.

"Sunshine Of Your Love," "White Room," and "Badge" (co-written by Capton and his friend George Harrison) are real

gems in Clapton's early career. In 1968, at the height of their success, Cream split up. Immediately afterwards, Clapton's

life acquired an irregular, nomadic pace. First he founded Blind Faith, with Ginger Baker and another friend, Steve

Winwood. "Presence Of The Lord" was this band's manifesto, but they cut only one record. The Delaney and Bonnie and

Friends adventure followed.

THE LEGENDARY
GUITAR
OF THE PRINCE
OF BRIT BLUES

Eric Clapton

151 [ERIC CLAPTON, 1983] ▲ The 1980s saw Eric Clapton's return to real blues and the acoustic guitar.

In 1970 Eric Clapton formed Derek & The Dominoes. By pure chance, another guitar genius joined the band: Duane Allman, leader of The Allman Brothers Band. The masterpiece recording *Layla & Other Assorted Love Songs* was the result. "Layla," with a sumptuous opening riff, is perhaps still the English guitarist's most famous song. The ensuing planetary success led to a tour, a live recording, and then . . . nothing. Duane Allman died in a motorcycle accident on the eve of their American tour, a second album failed before release, and Clapton found himself in the throes of heavy drug hell. It took many months and the help of friends like Pete Townshend and Jimmy Page to drag him back from the precipice, at least in part. His return was celebrated with a huge tour that ended at the Rainbow Theatre in London, resulting in a historic live album. Clapton got back on track and with *461 Ocean Boulevard* he was once again rumbling for fans from radios and record players. The first single, "I Shot the Sheriff," was a cover of a song by a then-unknown Jamaican artist named Bob Marley.

152-153 [THE YARDBIRDS, 1964] - Eric Clapton (second from the right to) joined the Yardbirds in 1963, and stayed with them until 1965.

153 [THE BLUESBREAKERS, 1966] - Clapton's career continued with the Blues Breakers, a real melting pot of blues talent. In the photo, from the left: John Mayall, Hughie Flint, Eric Clapton and John McVie.

The Eighties were a busy time for the guitarist, on the music scene and elsewhere. The early Nineties were a more tranquil period for Clapton, until life presented Clapton with the biggest bill a father could be asked to pay: his small son Conor, who was only four, died in a terrible accident. Clapton was shattered by the tragedy, and expressed his grief in a song dedicated to his dead child, "Tears in Heaven," which became a worldwide success. It was during this time of mourning that Clapton finally discovered his true love once more: the blues.

SLOWHAND

The recording of the disc *Unplugged*, for the TV show by the same name, was an opportunity to open his heart to the public and expose his wounds, as well as his strength and his love of the blues. His recent albums, his appearances alongside many other great artists, and his inspiration always drawn from the blues — and it is from the genre that he rarely strays. Able to express through music his uniquely personal style and human frailty, Clapton is in a totally individual dimension. What more could there be for a musician?

154 [SLOWHAND, 1977] - The image is taken from Eric Clapton's "Slowhand" album, the nickname most commonly used to describe the blues musician. The record contains some of his most famous songs including: "Cocaine?", "Wonderful Tonight" and "Lay Down Sally".

155 [ERIC CLAPTON] - Clapton dedicated himself to the blues throughout the 1990s, producing some of his most successful records: "Unplugged" in 1992 and the moving "From the Cradle" (2001).

Frank Vincent Zappa (December 21, 1940 – December 4, 1993). A mixed breed of European and Middle-Eastern

origins, of great intellectual passions, great political and cultural lucidity, Zappa was, despite all his excesses, a genius of the

Sixties and Seventies. Named in his honor after his death were two asteroids (3834 Zappafrank and 16745 Zappa); a gene

(the *Proteus mirabilis* gene is called ZapA); an extinct mollusk (*Amauratoma zappa*); and a spider whose abdomen has

markings that resemble the musician's famous moustache (*Pachygnatha zappa*). There was also a bronze statue by the

same sculptor commissioned for the monument to Lenin erected in Lithuania. During his lifetime he testified before the

American Senate during the Parents Music Resource Center debate, which sought to censor the freedom of artistic

speech and was viewed by many artists as a new form of McCarthyism. Above all this, he created a variant of pop that is

unequalled. In the footsteps of Varese and always using cutting edge technologies, mixing life, fiction and music, he trans-

ferred the cut-up (editing of pasted together fragments) from literature to pop. The first albums, like *Absolutely Free*

(1967) and *We're Only In It For The Money* (1968), describe hypocritical, conformist American society, the battle to destroy

free underground culture, and at the same time, also unmask the hypocrisies of the new symbols of the culture that was

THE ART

turning into a business (hippies, flower power and what was to become the Woodstock industry). Both the title (*We're Only*

OF SURPRISE

In It For The Money) and the cover, a parody of The Beatles' *Sgt. Pepper's Lonely Hearts Club Band,* were absolutely

AND ROCK

explicit in their references.

NO LIMITS

Frank Zappa

158 [FRANK ZAPPA, 1967] - The artist was involved in ongoing creative research and experimentation, also influenced by the provocation of the Theater of the Absurd.

158-159 [MOTHERS OF INVENTION, 1967] - Frank Zappa was the guitarist and leader of The Mothers of Invention, a rock band active from 1965 to 1975.

A genius of the guitar and a great producer and composer, Zappa left an immense musical legacy to be explored, much still hidden and all illuminated by a intellect that was lyrical and farsighted, when it was not obscured by its polemic trait. He had almost a philosophical attitude to music, the absolute liberty of being and playing without barriers or boundaries. Radical sounds were sewn into musical contexts never touched on by other pop musicians, in a sort of stylistic nomadism across all the territories he defined "conceptual continuity;" pop melodies were woven into jazz and virtuoso instrumentals; sequences of sounds and fragments of conversation were attached to extraordinary music. Zappa painted panoramas that surpassed sound to become culture. From "Louie Louie," which appears in more than 20 recordings as a riff, TV themes and rock songs like "My Sharona" or "Stairway to Heaven"; even Stravinsky: it was all fair game.

158, 159 Frank Zappa

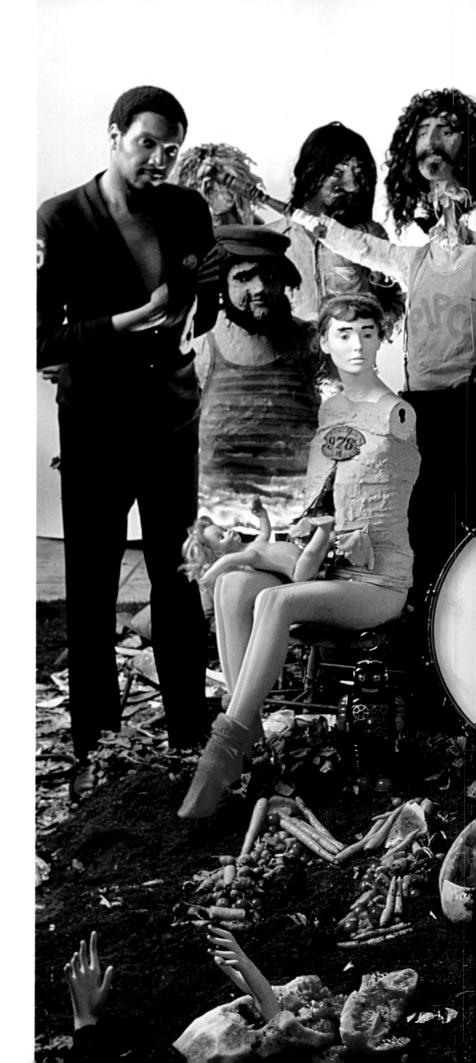

FRANK ZAPPA, 1979] – The American musician poses against the backdrop using the cover of the album "Sheik Yerbouti."

The Yellow Shark is the extraordinary final opus by the Great Desecrator. Despite the illness with which he had been diagnosed three years before he died, he managed a well-received public performance of this suite, put together with musical excerpts that belonged to various periods of his artistic life, and played in a classical vein. Zappa's concerts with the Ensemble Modern in 1992 were a real event for the conservative world of classical music. A rock composer speaking in the tongue of the classics and proposing a sort of fragmentary yet coherent "suite," using a quite personal linguistic crossover (linked to both his previous thirty years of work in rock and to the development of classic post-Schoenberg language) was not a common or easily digestible event. The Ensemble's immaculate rendition empowers Zappa's skill for constructing scores, and allows the referenced substrata to emerge – Webern, Stravinsky, Ligeti, Varèse, Bartok – as twentieth-century classical music as read and experienced through the Zappa composition. These final compositions may not be the favorite listening of those who prefer Zappa's histrionics as a satirist, or his fluid, errant guitar solos, but they are definitely worthy products that delve into the depths of the restless soul of a musician who was totally immersed in such a complex century. Frank Zappa is buried in Westwood Village Memorial Park Cemetery, Westwood, California.

▲ 2

1. and 2. One of the most complex, intriguing, interesting and difficult figures in the history of rock, Frank Zappa was always well-known for his eccentricity and irreverent expressive style.

Saturday, July 2, 2005, was the date of Live 8, the great musical event organized by Bob Geldof to raise public awareness

of Africa's poverty and other issues. Pink Floyd got back together specially and appeared with the historic line-up (with Roger

Waters) to play four iconic pieces from their vast repertoire: "Breathe," "Money," "Wish You Were Here," and "Comfortably

Numb." During the performance of "Wish You Were Here," Waters paid homage to his friend and the band's first leader, Syd

Barrett: "It's actually quite emotional, standing up here with these three guys after all these years. Standing up to be counted with

the rest of you. Anyway, we're doing this for everyone who's not here, particularly, of course, for Syd." The story of this unique

band of giants begins in a distant, yet memorable past. After playing) a series of concerts under a number of different names

(Sigma 6 and The Abdabs were two of them), at the UFO Club, a London temple of underground music, Pink Floyd became

famous. Their notoriety was especially linked to Syd Barrett's surreal lyrics (particulary on "Arnold Layne," "Bike," "See Emily

Play," "The Gnome," and "Scarecrow") and "space" music ("Interstellar Overdrive," "Astronomy Domine"), accompanied during

concerts by special visual effects (light, videos, etc). Pink Floyd cut two records with Syd Barrett *The Piper at The Gates of Dawn*

and *A Saucerful of Secrets* (in the latter Barrett actually only played on one track), after which he left the band for physical and

mental health problems thought to have been caused by his abuse of drugs. Gilmour was called upon first to support and then to

replace Barrett, with Pink Floyd then reaching the maturity that led them to produce Dark Side of The Moon. Subsequently a

FOUR EXPLORERS SEEKING

further crisis arose following the departure of Roger Waters in the early Eighties, until the recent regrouping.

THE DARK SIDE OF THE MOON

The classic Pink Floyd era began with the movie *Pink Floyd Live At Pompeii*, which was released in 1972 but is still a

memorable cinematic moment both for the performance in an empty theatrical space and for the audio and visual effects used,

totally immersed in the era's psychedelic and sci-fi culture. It continued with *Dark Side of the Moon* (1973) and *Wish You Were*

Here (released in 1975 and including the classic "Shine On You Crazy Diamond," a tribute to Syd Barrett).

Pink Floyd

165 [MADISON SQUARE GARDEN, 1987] ⏶ One of Pink Floyd's last great world tours also played a gig in New York.

166 [LONDON, 1967] - The group's founder members have their photo taken as they leap at hand down in front of EMI House, London.

167 [PINK FLOYD, 1966] - From the left: Roger Waters, Nick Mason, Syd Barrett and Richard Wright.

168-169 [PINK FLOYD] - Pink Floyd at Los Angeles Sport Arena in 1980, with the album "The Wall," released in 1979.

In 1979 they released the rock opera *The Wall*, which garnered critical praise and reached the number one spot on the US album chart. In 1982, it was made into a movie that featured Bob Geldof as the main character, a disillusioned rock star called Pink, a character based loosely on both Roger Waters (who wrote the film's screenplay) and Syd Barrett. The film's disturbing visuals and non-linear storyline did not keep ticket-buyers away; the film was very successful in the US and ultimately won two BAFTA awards in the UK.

Roger Waters left the band in 1985 after the release of The Final Cut, and David Gilmour took over the de facto leader of the band. During the Gilmour era the band went on a successful world tour that included an unforgettable show at the Venice Lagoon and spawned the live album *Delicate Sound of Thunder* (1988). In 1994 *The Division Bell* was released. This was the band's last studio work and marked the creative return of Richard Wright (he had rejoined the band during the recording of Momentary Lapse of Reason, but admittedly made minimal contributions). The next year P*U*L*S*E was released. A compendium of live performances from September 1994 at venues in London, Rome, Hanover, and Modena, the album boasts the first full live version of *Dark Side of the Moon*. Psychedelic dreams, avant-garde electronics, progressive rock: some say it all started with Pink Floyd. Though Syd Barrett has been lost (he died July 7, 2006), Barrett's shadow, as testified by Waters' words at Live 8, will always linger. The "Crazy Diamond" watches over his favorite child.

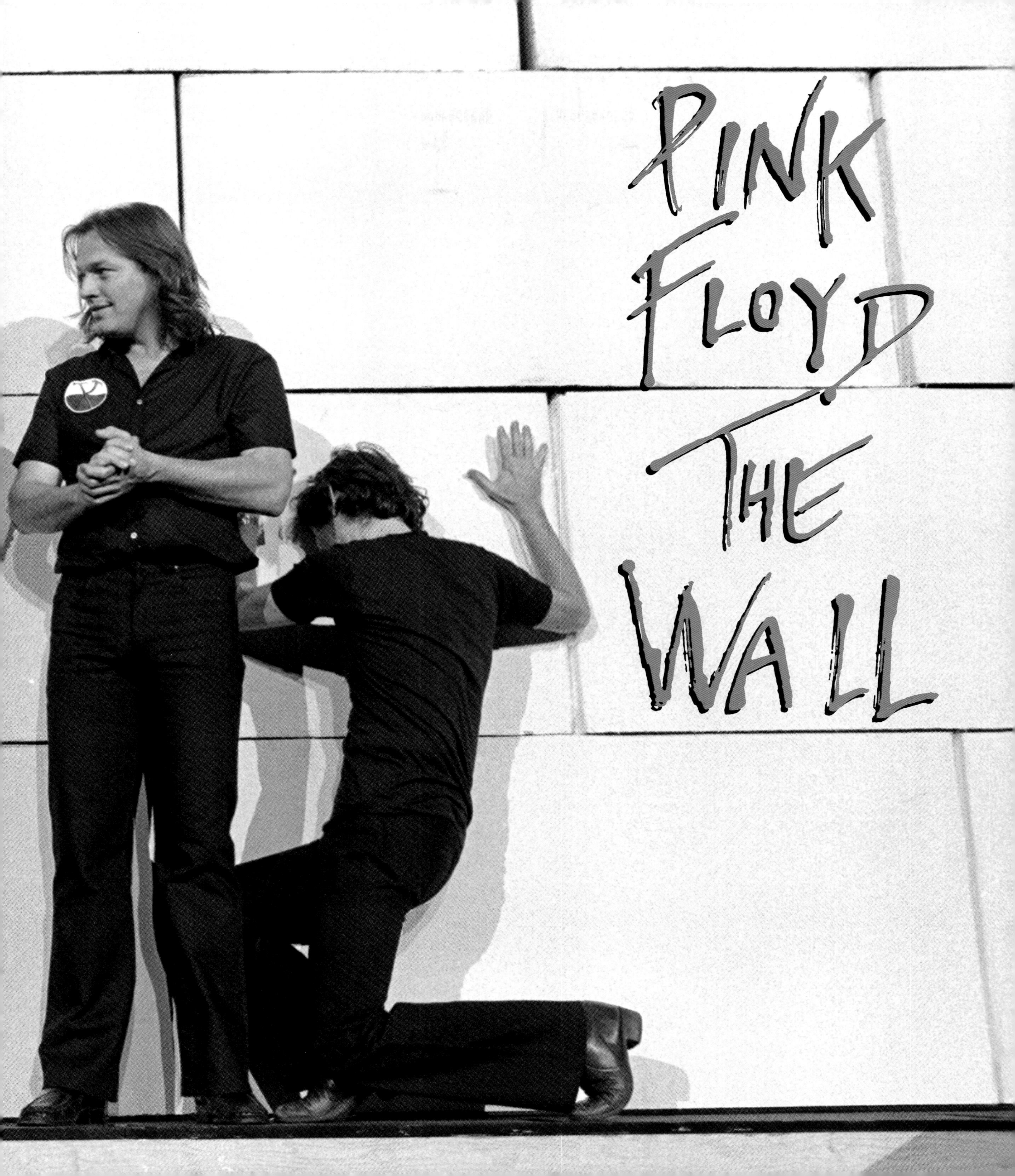
PINK FLOYD
THE WALL

[CONCERT, 1994] - In 1994 Pink Floyd took to stage again to promote a new album: "The Division Bell."

The legendary Mexican guitarist Carlos Augusto Alves Santana was born in 1947, in Autlan de Navarro, Jalisco, Mexico. His father was violinist, and passed on the love of music to his eldest son. His family moved to Tijuana, Mexico when Carlos was 8, and sometimes played violin with his father's mariachi band, and later played bass in dancehalls, where he came to know BB King's blues and Little Richard's rock. Carlos emigrated to San Francisco when he was 13, but was not impressed with the popular music of the time. Gradually, Carlos found the local blues scene in San Francisco, and the rest is history. He has never retired from the stage and seems in even better shape and more creative now than ever. There is a Santana with his historic Woodstock line-up, who produced three initial masterpieces: *Santana*, *Abraxas*, and *Santana III*. From 1971 to the present day the band has changed members more than 40 times. Then there is Santana with his parallel solo career, where he has always experimented through rock, jazz, and Latino music, creating an identifiable and unique mix that led to the worldwide success of *Supernatural* in 1999, selling 23 million copies and wining nine Grammy Awards, breaking down any and all barriers of genre and audience. He ran the gamut from rock hero to pop hero, not to mention his forays into the mystical on his records with John Mc Laughlin and the live works like the gigantic *Lotus* in the Seventies, which combined jazz, rock, and flamenco. Santana finally came full circle and returned the blues as a guest musician on the last two

THE LATINO

albums recorded in the Eighties and Nineties by the famous bluesman John Lee Hooker: *Chill Out* and *The Healer*.

HEART OF ROCK

Santana

174 [SANTANA-LYON, 1969] - The image shows the cover of a record released by Carlos Santana in 1969 under the Columbia Records label.

175 [ST. OUEN, 1981] - The Mexican musician shown during a guitar solo at the St Ouen concert in France.

176 [SANTANA] - Carlos Santana and his band in the 1980s.

177 [SANTANA LIVE] - Santana's music has always experimented with various genres: salsa, classic rock, blues and fusion, putting together a unique and unmistakable style.

In 2005, now an icon of international music and a revered guitar-playing hero, Santana, released the 38th album of his monumental career, *All That I Am*, his third album for Arista Records, featuring numerous excellent guest players: Steven Tyler, Michelle Branch & The Wreckers, OutKast's Big Boi, Mary J. Blige, Metallica's Kirk Hammett, Sean Paul, Los Lonely Boys, Joss Stone, will.i.am, Anthony Hamilton, Bo Bice and Robert Randolph.

All That I Am is the continuation of the artistic vision of Carlos Santana and Clive Davis, with whom he has worked since the Columbia Records days, during his initial rise to success more than 30 years ago. His is an artistic vision that has never been contradicted, never betrayed. In this aspect, Santana stands as an extraordinary exception, a great musician true to his music, his life and his style, endowed with a great personality and great spirituality, gracefully surviving the shipwreck of an entire generation of his contemporaries.

Carlos Santana has won ten Grammy awards, has sold over 90 million records and has performed for more than 100 million people. Since his historic, electrifying apparition at Woodstock in 1969, Carlos has grown into a universally famous artist, one who continues to evolve and grow in each new production. His life has been one of the most extraordinary and creative musical journeys ever undertaken: long and lovely, like the infinite notes that pour from his guitar.

178 [CARLOS SANTANA IN CONCERT] - The musician has used various guitars during his career: a Yamaha SG2000, that acquired the nickname "Santana model," a Gibson SG and a Paul Reed Smith.

179 [TOUR 2002] - Carlos Santana performing at the Shoreline Amphitheater during the tour for the "Shaman" album.

It was a brief season, the summer of 1965: Lambrettas and Vespas were the choice for the weekend ride

to Brighton. Kids were smartly dressed (but also wore parkas to keep out the cold), their pockets filled with

amphetamines to keep awake through Saturday and Sunday, dancing till they dropped to the black beats they

preferred. It was the summer that saw the birth of The Who and which hallmarked them for their entire exis-

tence. They were Mods. They had rock 'n' roll dreams, reveries of social emancipation, and were full of cul-

tural tumult and rage against a throwaway society that marginalized them, and desperation for the years of

youth slipping fast away and forcing a swift defeat. "Hope I die before I get old" they screamed; Keith Moon

(just about) succeeded.

They appeared at the Monterey Pop Festival in 1967, and at Woodstock in 1969. Their fame as "the"

Mod band of 1965 and 1966, was later described in *Quadrophenia* (the 1973 album and 1979 movie starring,

amongst others, The Police's Sting).

WHEN ROCK
WAS SAVED
BY TOWNSHEND
AND DALTREY

The Who

181 [THE WHO, 1969] ▲ Pete Townshend, the band's guitarist seen leaping across the stage during a 1969 concert at the Tanglewood Summer "Contemporary Tends," in Lenox, Massachusetts.

The band was the brainchild of Pete Townshend (guitar and writer of most of their songs), Roger Daltrey (vocals), John Entwistle (bass), and Keith Moon (drums). *My Generation* (1965), *A Quick One* (1966), *Who Sell Out* (1967) are the records that made them famous. "My Generation," like The Stones' "Satisfaction" or Dylan's "Like a Rolling Stone," describes the disquiet of the young, and became their anthem. *Tommy* (1969), *Live at Leeds* (1970), *Who's Next* (1971), and *Quadrophenia* (1973), are more mature works, where the the band's furious energies seen in live performances like that at Woodstock combine with Townshend's writing and descriptive talents. *Tommy* became a successful movie (Tina Turner's version of "Acid Queen" is famous).

182 [THE WHO, 1969] - The band was founded in 1964 by Keith Moon (drums, left), Pete Townshend (guitarist and author), John Entwistle (electric bass) and Roger Daltrey (vocalist).

183 [PARIS, 1960s] - The rock band hit the European musical scenario in the mid-1960s, with an album called "My Generation."

184 [CONCERT, USA, 1975] - In 1975 "The Who by Numbers" was released, with many tracks influenced by a narrative style.

185 [THE WHO, 1982 AND 1972] - The Who performing (here seen in the USA, respectively in 1982, top, and 1972 bottom) discharged terrific energy that sometimes channeled into broken guitars and risky high jumps.

In 1978 they were featured in a documentary entitled *The Kids Are Alright*. The Who, contemporaries of The Beatles and Rolling Stones, influenced a long list of people with their music: Led Zeppelin, the punk wave, U2, Oasis. Keith Moon died in 1978 and John Entwistle in 2002, but Townshend and Daltrey live on, continuing to perform their classic songs, accompanied by Pino Palladino on bass and Zak Starkey (son of Richard, aka The Beatles' Ringo Starr) on drums. This lineup of The Who played at Live 8 on 2 July 2005.

[LOS ANGELES, 1980] - Several fans of The Who wearing a band T-shirt during a 1980 concert.

The cover of The Who album
"Tommy," which inspired the rock
opera of the same name and later
a film.

They were four successful musicians: David Crosby (the guitarist for The Byrds, songwriter and vocalist); Stephen Stills (vocalist and guitarist with Buffalo Springfield and, later for Manassas); Graham Nash (songwriter, guitarist and keyboards with British group The Hollies); Neil Young (songwriter and guitarist with Buffalo Springfield and, later for Crazy Horse; perhaps most successful as a solo artist; present at several concerts with Bob Dylan's Traveling Wilburys).

They released three albums: *Crosby, Stills and Nash*, 1969; *Déjà Vu* (with Young), 1970; *Four Way Street* (with Young), 1971.

They are legendary and there are no signs of their greatness diminishing. There have been a number of comebacks; most recently was in the spring of 2005 for several concerts in the US.

They have released countless discs amongst themselves, as solo artists, duos, or trios; an infinity of concerts, but what comes to mind is always the sparks at the 1967 Monterey Pop Festival when Crosby played several pieces with Buffalo Springfield; a few months later he left The Byrds. Things went rather faster and further, however, when a personal hero of theirs appeared on the scene: Graham Nash, the leader of The Hollies, touring in California. The mix was explosive, in just a month they wrote and recorded the perfect album, Crosby, *Stills and Nash* that is still surprising today.

HEARTS, GUITARS AND SONGS FROM 1970s CALIFORNIA

Crosby, Stills, Nash & Young

Vocal harmonies, acoustic guitars, production that is so crystal-clear it could be digital – a legend was born. Neil Young was recalcitrant but increasingly drawn, and in the end he left Buffalo Springfield and joined the supergroup, making his debut with them at Woodstock, no less: a perfect strategy or just a magic destiny? With Young, the band became strong, political, a bridge between Californian utopian ideals and the radical pacifist *movement*. They became leaders of the anti-Vietnam movement, which was making its voice felt in American colleges, challenging police repression, and which at Woodstock counted on the presence of Dylan, a reluctant symbol of a generation that crowned first Hendrix and then Neil Young. *Déjà Vu* was the perfect second record, the songs rolling one into the other, describing the disparity between the American dream and the American reality. Their classic take on rock music was like a Botticelli painting: there are not too many details, no excesses, just what's necessary. The road called, but after the tour in the summer of 1970, the group fell apart. Luckily for their fans, they had recorded enough live material for a third album, the magnificent *Four Way Street*, which for years fed the imaginations of all those who missed seeing them play together; those who have chased the ghosts of the legend in each musician's individual concerts and records, in the vain hope of an impossible reunion. The album also contains, amongst others, Neil Young's famous protest song, "Ohio," in memory of the 1970 massacre at Kent State University in Ohio, when police shot into a crowd of anti-war demonstrators, killing four unarmed students. The song became a manifesto against the US involvement in the Vietnam War.

192 [BACKSTAGE, 1970] - A close-up of musician David Crosby, before a USA concert; Neil Young can be seen in the background.

193 top [CROSBY, STILLS & NASH, 1969] - The group on the road (from the left): Stephen Stills (with a camera), David Crosby, Joni Mitchell and Graham Nash.

193 center and bottom [TOUR 1974] - The group before and during the 1974 concert in San Francisco. Neil Young (centre of the top photograph) has joined the line-up for the Woodstock Festival.

191 [CROSBY, STILLS, NASH AND YOUNG] ▲ The popular American pop/rock band line-up was (from the left): David Crosby, Stephen Stills, Graham Nash and Neil Young.

194-195 [CROSBY, STILLS & NASH, 1969] - A shot of the founder members (Nash, Stills and Crosby) used for the cover of their first album "Crosby, Stills and Nash," released in 1969.

196 [STEPHEN STILLS] - Vocalist, guitarist and composer who was part of the CSN&Y quartet. He later went solo, as did the rest of the band.

197 [NEIL YOUNG] - The musician, after he joined the Crosby, Stills & Nash trio for the albums "Déjà Vu" and "Four Way Street," went solo and, in 1972, shot to the top of the US charts with his "Harvest" album.

To experience their songs they should be heard, of course, but here we can but mention them, like the stations of a cross representing joy, revolution, dreams, utopia, pain; but never "surrender." Here they are: "Teach your Children," "The Lee Shore," "Suite Judy Blue Eyes," "Carry On," "Right Between the Eyes," "Love the One You're With," and their version of Joni Mitchell's "Woodstock."

The Seventies and the decades to follow, saw the four in flight from their own legend — an impossible flight given the huge burden that recorded history continues to lay on the doorstep of that short, intense experience.

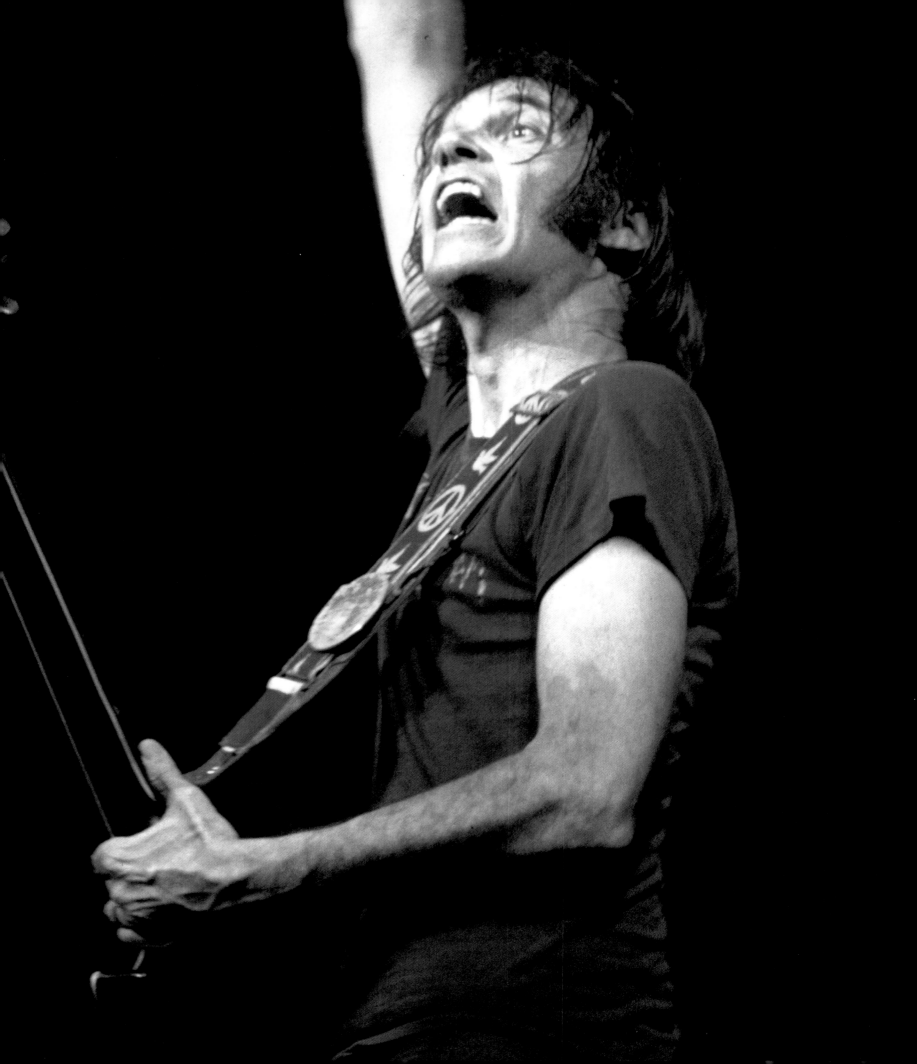

1. and 2. Neil Young in concert. The Canadian singer-songwriter has always successfully renewed his musical inspiration and retained his individuality, even as part of the groups with whom he worked, and has been part of the rock scene for four decades.

From 1965 to 1968, London saw the future members of Deep Purple present in various groups that followed the musical taste of the time, varying from mimicking The Beatles to being influenced by the California sound. Eventually they met and formed a band that shocked the world of music by creating a sort of very "hard" rock, defined as "heavy metal" (a term coined by the Steppenwolf song, "Born to be Wild," which at one point talks of "heavy metal thunder"), as were the early works of Black Sabbath. In October 1968 the group had a huge US success with the single "Hush," a cover of a Joe South song, and with their debut album *Shades of Deep Purple*. Since then, Deep Purple have established themselves as one of the most important and famous bands on the international scene, releasing a series of albums between 1970 and 1972 that were enormous hits and had a deep impact on rock music: *Deep Purple in Rock*, *Fireball* and *Machine Head* (which included their most famous song of all, "Smoke on the Water," inspired by the fire at the Montreux Casino that destroyed all of Frank Zappa and The Mothers of Invention's equipment). In addition to the three studio albums, there was a live double album, *Made in Japan*, probably the most famous for hard rock and heavy metal genres.

The classic lineup lasted until the release of the album *Who Do We Think We Are* (1973), after which Gillan and Glover left the band and were replaced by an unknown vocalist, David Coverdale, with Glenn Hughes on bass and as backup voice. With this lineup another successful record was cut in 1974, titled *Burn*. Then legendary guitarist Ritchie Blackmore also left the group, to found Rainbow. With them he played classic Deep Purple rock around the world.

THE GREAT FATHERS OF BRITISH HARD ROCK

Deep Purple

201 [NEW YORK, 1998] ⬆ Ian Gillan and Steve Morse during a performance at Jones Beach Amphitheater, New York, 1998.

202 AND 203 [DEEP PURPLE, 1973] - The hard rock band during a 1973 concert. The line-up included Ritchie Blackmore (top photo), Glenn Hughes on bass and Jon Lord on keyboards (photo right), entering the world of rock with a very unique style to become a seminal heavy metal band.

In April 1984, Deep Purple finally got back together. During BBC Radio's Friday Rock Show it was announced that the group's classic lineup (Blackmore, Gillan, Glover, Lord, and Paice) were starting to produce new material. The group signed a contract with Polydor for Europe, and with Mercury for North America. The album *Perfect Strangers* was released in October and followed by a world tour, starting in New Zealand and closing in Europe. It was a huge success.

Despite being remembered overall as pioneers of heavy metal, Deep Purple were never a band typical of this genre, both in the talent of each musician and in the themes they covered in their music. The group always adapted its style to the various lineups, preferring a virtuoso technique for each member as the chief characteristic and source of inspiration.

The influence of classical music (especially Lord's contributions) was easy to pinpoint, as was the presence of flamenco in Blackmore's solos, and various pieces include jazz, rhythm 'n' blues, and soul elements. Deep Purple are sometimes classified as progressive rock, alongside groups like Yes or Genesis for their great creativity and capacity for innovation on a musical plane, and for their evident aspiration to create art rock. Certainly this is applicable to the group's earliest work like *The Book of Taliesyn*, in the late Sixties.

For a number of years, Ian Gillan, who sang Jesus in the original 1970 recording of Andrew Lloyd Webber and Tim Rice's *Jesus Christ Superstar*, was rock's point-of-reference vocalist, alongside Led Zeppelin's Robert Plant. Gillan's formidable extension and his performance of "Child In Time"– a performance worthy of a soprano — will remain one of the truly unique sound images of rock.

[IAN PAICE, 1976] - Ian Paice was the band's only drummer and was the only musician to be present in all of the line-ups. ◄

Yes

Yes is one of the most famous groups in progressive rock. They formed in London in 1968, when Jon Anderson met Chris Squire by chance in the pub where he was working as a barman while awaiting his chance to get into the worldwide music scene. Squire played bass in a band called Mabel Greer's Toyshop and asked Anderson to come on board as a vocalist. The group also included keyboard player Tony Kaye and drummer Bill Bruford. Guitarist Peter Banks also joined, but left in 1970 and was replaced by the highly talented Steve Howe, who profoundly changed the sound of the band.

In August 1971, Tony Kaye left the group and was replaced by another virtuoso, The Strawbs' keyboard player Rick Wakeman (who turned down offers from David Bowie and Lou Reed to join Yes). Wakeman was a marvelous soloist and soon proved to be the perfect foil for Howe. He also introduced two new key elements to the group's range of instruments: the Mellotron and the Minimoog. The first recording by the "classic" Yes lineup (Anderson, Bruford, Howe, Squire. and Wakeman) was a 10-minute performance of the Paul Simon classic "America."

It was at this time that the band met Eddie Offord, a well-known producer who later went down in rock history precisely for his work with groups like Yes and Emerson Lake and Palmer. In March 1971, the band released their third opus, *The Yes Album*, which was their first with Howe and Offord and decreed their ascent into the Olympus of rock. The album

ROCK MEETS
shot to the top of the UK charts and sold well abroad too; by April, Yes went on tour for the first time in the United States,
THE CLASSICS
supporting Jethro Tull.

Yes

207 [STEVE HOWE, 1970] ▲
Few people know that Howe turned
down the chance to be Jethro Tull's
solo guitar to join Yes.

208 [LIVE, 1977] - The rock band in concert in the USA in 1977. The late 1970s were a transition period for them: solo experiments, new keyboard player and a new way of conceiving live performances as all-round shows.

209 [RICK WAKEMAN, 1974] - The Yes keyboard player enjoyed a turbulent relationship with the band. The tall man (he is over 6' 2") of British rock is said to have left and come back four times.

The style of the band appeared complete and mature. In the period immediately after this, Yes recorded two milestones of progressive rock, *Fragile* in 1971 and *Close to the Edge* in 1972. Both enjoyed great chart success, both in Europe and in America, and were followed by world tours. *Fragile* also marked the start of a long association between Yes and painter Roger Dean, who created most of the group's album covers and the choreographies used in concerts.

Not long after the release of *Close to the Edge*, Bruford left Yes to join King Crimson. He was replaced by Alan White, who was the former drummer for John Lennon's Plastic Ono Band. White made his appearance on vinyl in 1972 in the monumental live triple album *Yessongs*.

It's pointless to list the band's numerous lineups or albums; the band's music, even in the worst moments of the Eighties and Nineties, although marked by the huge success of songs like "Owner of a Lonely Heart," never strayed too far from the classic Yes sound. Yes is still active and has a huge following at an international level: the last album (a live album, called *The Word is Live*) was released in 2005 and was preceded by a world tour that touched all five continents. In over 35 years of their career, the group has changed members numerous times. For now Yes has returned to what most fans would acknowledge as the "classic" lineup: Jon Anderson on vocals, Steve Howe on guitar, Chris Squire on bass, Rick Wakeman on keyboards, and Alan White on drums.

Just like the Pied Piper of Hamelin fairytale, Jethro Tull's flute charmed listeners and enticed them to follow the piper. When Scotsman Ian Anderson's flute was playing "Living In The Past," the combination of the magical, ancient sound vibrating through the air and the musician's breath bursting continuously into the instrument's sound, formed an oneiric, mysterious dimension that became almost an obsession for millions of rock fans worldwide. For the first time in rock, the classical sound of the transverse flute became an unprecedented source of musical energy. Jethro Tull was Ian Anderson's successful experiment. From folk, through blues, towards rock, Tull walked the line that connected four worlds simultaneously, with different balances in the various phases of their lengthy life.

Stand Up, released in 1969, was Anderson and Co.'s first real success and it went down in history mainly for the revisitation of Bach's *Bourée*. However, the record also presents pieces that go back to Tull roots: "A New Day Yesterday" (blues), "Jeffrey Goes to Leicester Square" (folk), and the rock ballads "We Used to Know" and "Reasons for Waiting."

The key to their success was not only the group's well-defined style, but also the flute-playing and personality of Ian Anderson. His instrumental and improvisational ability sprang from the live side of the double *Living in the Past* album.

ROCK, JAZZ, BALLADS AND SONGS

Jethro Tull

212 [*AQUALUNG* 1971]- The cover of the album released in 1971.

211 [JETHRO TULL IN CONCERT] ▲ Folk and rock fusing in a live show by Jethro Tull, with founder Ian Anderson and guitarist Martin Barre.

213 [JAN ANDERSON IN CONCERT] - Multi-talented musician and vocalist, Anderson was also the author of the lyrics and music of most of Jethro Tull's songs.

The group left the Sixties with confused ideas about what their place in the world of music really was, excluded from large-scale events and followed only by their faithful fans. In addition, Ian Anderson's awkward, exuberant personality, which gave the group its shine on stage, made relations with the press and the public rather cool, and didn't encourage positive group-media or group-fans communications.

Benefit seemed to be the end, but 1971's *Aqualung* took the public and the critics by surprise. *Aqualung* is still the band's manifesto, their perfect record. The blues and rock moods are back, alternating with folk episodes with biting political lyrics, which contributed to making "Aqualung" Jethro Tull's most famous single. The fame of Ian Anderson and his mates resounded around the world and Tull became real superstars; Anderson's pelican pose as he performed his famous solos made him a rock icon. With *Thick as a Brick*, a single great suite, and an excellent example of great impact and musical merit, Tull confirmed their legend and began their decline. Unknowingly, *Thick as a Brick* was a swan song, because the group failed to repeat its success and the general public slowly abandoned them.

In the Eighties, the group rode the wave of long international tours, mixing hard sound (as in *Rock Island*) with electronic contaminations, but the substance no longer changed and from that time onwards, Tull became a "working" band, always welcome at concerts. Their last record with new material was released in 1999, and on it fans found echoes of the sounds that entranced so many years before.

1. and 2. Anderson the "pied piper." The Scots musician's flute is a hallmark of his melodies and the group's image, inspiring numerous other artists.

▲ 3

▲ 4

3. and 4. Vocalist and multi-instrumentalist who turns his hand to harmonica, electric and bass guitar, sax, keyboards, drums, Hammond organ, trombone and violin.

Perhaps the most succinct, complete, efficacious, and true written portrait of David Bowie appeared in the now-historic 1983 *Rolling Stone Rock 'n' Roll Encyclopedia*. The entry dedicated to the British musician began with this incisive summary: "David Bowie has made his career a series of charged, contradictory images – androgynous, alien, decadent, star, fashion plate, traveler – while making increasingly avant-garde music. He has drawn on freely-acknowledged sources, from Marc Bolan to the Velvet Underground to Brian Eno, put his own mark on them, then abruptly moved on, leaving behind imitators of each of his phases."

With Bowie the classic rock era ended, in the sense that Bowie arrived while historic rock was losing its motivations and its creators. Bowie arrived in time to pick up a few scraps of this music, which was changing its skin, and he grafted the new into that, facing the future. It was not the only time he did it: he returned in the mid-Seventies with new constructs, joining forces with two other creative figures of the British scene: Brian Eno and Robert Fripp, and together they inaugurated a new and more revolutionary rock era.

MR JONES AND HIS
THOUSAND MASKS

David Bowie

If Bowie had a virtue at the end of the Sixties, it was that he reacted to the identity crisis affecting rock as a culture and as a generation of musicians, after the Woodstock jag and the loss of a series of guiding lights who were mowed down by heroin abuse, as the Sixties slid into the Seventies.

A quick recap: there was Woodstock, but there was also the disbanding of The Beatles. There the conquest of the moon and the inevitable rush to technological modernization under the double thrust of the USA-USSR space challenge and the war in Vietnam. (And it was this modernization that brought inflation and a mid-Seventies crisis, which set the stage the premise for the new Eighties modernization.) All of this was off-set by the youth protests that refused to make the societal values absolute: in America the anti-Vietnam movement took hold, as did the civil rights movement; in Europe the clash was more about ideology, with the '68 legends and Third World heroes battling against capitalism. In London, from 1969 to 1971, there were plenty of drugs, lots of pacifist and black-out culture, lots of Orient, and a great deal of the dregs of psychedelia.

This was the scenario where Bowie was initially a walk-on and then turned into a catalyst. Bowie was undecided between Velvet Underground and Stones-style heroin-soaked decadence (the post-Brian Jones Stones), or Pink Floyd's psychedelic trips towards an electronic-mystic future, enhanced by the colors of LSD. So in the end he sort of found a middle ground, got rid of his Mod gear, and with increasing authority turned into a musician who knew he was between a disappearing world and the dawn of a new world. The Sixties were on their way out (they didn't go away completely until '73 or '74) but at that time the Seventies seemed like some awful imitation, vulgar and impoverished. Bowie became the symbol of this indecision, this ambiguity, this loss of direction.

His style became increasingly evident in his records: first he took in Dylan, then Lou Reed, then The Stones, then Donovan, then psychedelia. After that, Bowie was born and even if "Man of Words, Man of Music" (then *Space Oddity*) isn't totally the sound of a musician with a personal style, the seeds of genius were certainly sown. "Space Oddity," the song that opens the album, is already a mature glance at the future. The rest of the album (and let's not forget Rick Wakeman's keyboards), is still in that sort of limbo between the past and the future from which many never managed to shake free. Bowie, on the other hand, spent the Eighties and Nineties reinventing himself – with some ups and downs – and pursuing his leader role, experimenting, sowing seeds for the future and then moving on, ever forward.

217 [USA, 1972] ▲ The British musician in a USA concert at the time of Ziggy Stardust.

218 [PORTRAIT, 1970] - Acoustic guitar and drab look: the phase preceding the androgynous costumes and oneiric stage outfits that made him famous.

220 [ALADDIN SANE, 1973] -
The cover of the first album
totally written and realized by
the artist, following an intense
American tour.

221 [1970] - The years when
Bowie reached a watershed in
his musical development,
following his meeting with
Mick Ronson. This was also
when he started to evolve his
image as well as stage
choreography effects, take his
cue from choreographer
Lindsay Kemp.

ALADDIN SANE

222 [DAVID BOWIE] - The 1980s change of look meant a more understated and minimal image, but his music changed too, transformed to a refined, generic pop.

223 [CHANGESONEBOWIE, 1976] - The cover for the compilation album of David Bowie hits, 1969-1976. The photo is by Tom Kelley, who had taken portraits of Marilyn Monroe.

222, 223 David Bowie

CHANGESONEBOWIE

224 AND 225 [LET'S DANCE, 1983] – The singer, in close-up and with his audience, during the "Serious Moonlight" tour, for the album "Let's Dance."

226-227 [DAVID BOWIE LIVE] - The singer performs on a raised stage wearing angel wings, late 1980s.

227 [DAVID BOWIE, 1987] - Bowie dancing
during a 1987 performance.

228 [CONCERT, 1980s] - In the 1980s Bowie
invested extensively in his acting career –
both films and theater – and invested in
some ostentatious tours.

Tony Banks (piano and keyboards), Peter Gabriel (vocalist and flute) were schoolmates at Charterhouse

School in Surrey. They met Anthony Phillips (guitarist) and Mike Rutherford (guitarist and bass), and that was,

well, the genesis. In 1969, with the album *From Genesis to Revelation* the group went public, narrating the history

of the world from creation to the present day – a debut that was bit over the top for some. Certainly that album

was the brainchild of naïve but ambitious students just out of college, that were keen to play music, but on their

own terms. A few people noticed them, but not very many. The subsequent *Trespass* (1970) showed that Genesis

was beginning to outline a musical style, and the group's live performances allowed Peter Gabriel plenty of

theatrical space. It was during that period that a series of concerts by this strange ensemble, appearing to be a

combination of Elizabethan theater and a Baroque quintet, brought Genesis to the notice of Italian music fans

before they were acknowledged by the British public. *Trespass*, lavish with innovative ideas and offbeat intuitions

in the composition ("Stagnation"), undescored how striking the quintet was. Thanks to *Trespass* the group began

PROGRESSIVE

to make headway in Northern Europe too, especially in Belgium and The Netherlands.

ROCK, A CLASSIC

OF ITS GENRE

Genesis & Peter Gabriel

In 1971 *Nursery Cryme* was released and caught the eye of critics and the general public, who all gave the group (now with former child actor Phil Collins on drums and a new guitarist, Steve Hackett, replacing Phillips) the thumbs up.

The title of the album was inspired by nursery rhymes, fairytales, and myths, which Gabriel and his companions narrate in a lovely musical fresco that may well be the group's most complete moment of artistic expression. Outstanding songs are "The Musical Box," "For Absent Friends," "Harold the Barrel," and "The Fountain of Salmacis." *Nursery Cryme* marked the start of a beautiful friendship between Genesis and Italy, the country that carried the band to some unforeseen success both in scope and intensity. They played terrific concerts that left spectators with a legacy of new, unforgettable emotions. From Italy, Genesis set off to conquer the world.

231 [PETER GABRIEL, 1988] ⏴ The vocalist and founder of Genesis performing in New Delhi, in 1988, for Amnesty International.

232 AND 233 [GENESIS LIVE] - Phil Collins, legendary Genesis drummer, took over as front man — becoming vocalist and leader for the band — when Peter Gabriel took his leave in 1975.

A year after *Foxtrot*, they released *Selling England by the Pound*. The album is a masterpiece. It opens with "… can you tell me where my country lies…" and even after listening to it repeatedly, you won't tire of it. In *Selling England* Genesis finally reached that ideal balance: the members of the band achieve the fusion of themselves and their musical ideas. The instrumentations, the lyrics, the overall sound, production, and cover, were the best that pop music had to offer. The record was a runaway hit and pushed Genesis into a vortex of musical-theatrical performances, where Gabriel reached the heights of the narrative dimension, acting on stage all the fantastic figures of his texts.

Then Gabriel and Genesis threw themselves into the most ambitious work of their career, *The Lamb Lies Down on Broadway*. Hearkening back to From *Genesis to Revelation*, this concept album is not set in the past or in the land of fables, but in 1974 New York.

234 AND 235 [PETER GABRIEL IN CONCERT] – Two images of the Genesis vocalist in the 1970s. His live performances were always renowned for their verve.

The story is that of Rael, who sprays his name on the city's walls, as if it is the only way he knows to express his personality. Feeling estranged from his bandmates, Peter Gabriel left the group after their next tour. Collins stepped into his shoes as Genesis vocalist, eventually steering the band in a new, more commercial direction. Genesis survived, changing lineup a number of times, following Collins amidst supergroups and pop success.

Peter Gabriel's focus was elsewhere. He dedicated his solo career to the music of non-European cultures, opening up to the rest of the world, making social and political statements against South African apartheid, writing music and songs in which all his youthful enthusiasm for Otis Redding and Nina Simone came to the fore.

The founders of Genesis were perfect sons of upper middle-class England. The original members of the band all came from nice British bourgeois families, and these roots were never rejected. They explored the roots of that culture and they played a musical game on the upper levels of pop culture, which explains their early success, first in Europe and then at home, and Gabriel's declining interest after several years. He'd said all there was to say about the dreams he dreamed on misty Surrey evenings, when school was out.

1. and 2. Peter Gabriel diving into the audience during the song "Lay Your Hands On Me"; Ivory Coast concert, 1988.

▴1

2

238-239 [GROWING-UP TOUR, 2003] - Peter Gabriel during the tour promoting his album "UP."

From Africa to America and back: this was an ancestral, spiritual and physical journey made by Bob Marley, observed by the world and by his people. Bob Marley was born in 1945, in Saint Ann, Jamaica. His mother was Jamaican and black and his father was British and white, but Marley opted to explore his Ethiopian roots on Jamaica's soil. First with ska, then with reggae, he spread awareness and pride, laying claim to justice and peace. After his death there was much speculation that his remains might be returned to Mother Africa, to whom he had dedicated his entire artistic existence and his last testimony as a musician, although this has not occurred. In point of fact, *Survival* (1979) was the spiritual testament of the great reggae-man: each song is almost a chapter of a book on Africa and its problems. It is also a book of prayers and dreams to realize for those who would come after him. Marley's political mysticism reached its peak in this last great album. Songs like "Survival," "So Much Trouble In The World," "Zimbabwe," and "Africa Unite" are unequalled in their musical inspiration and for the ethical greatness of the lyrics.

Marley's songs and person were the underpinning for the mass diffusion of reggae music outside of Africa. After various local productions in the Sixties, he signed a contract in 1971 with Chris Blackwell's Island Records – highly influential and innovative at that time.

THE PROPHET OF JAMAICAN MUSIC

Bob Marley & The Wailers

241 [PARIS, 1980] ▲ The reggae musician performing to an audience of 50,000 during the last concert of the 1980 French tour – Le Bourget, Paris.

242 [KINGSTON, 1980] - Bob Marley's cultural and artistic roots are embedded deep in Jamaican soil: a portrait as he relaxed in Kingston.

243 [THE WAILERS] - The band's original line-up, in London during the British tour for the album "Catch a Fire," released in 1973.

Island Records produced a large number of successful artists, including Genesis, John Martyn, and Nick Drake. Island elevated Marley to a world-famous icon and discs like *Natty Dread* (1975), followed by *Kaya* and *Rastaman Vibration*, right through to the live *Babylon By Bus* and his masterpiece, *Exodus* (1977), became memorable episodes of a unique career.

Marley was also known for his fervent Rastafarian religious beliefs and he actually became a Rasta missionary, bringing the faith to worldwide attention. He preached brotherhood and peace for all humanity, and was even baptized into the orthodox Ethiopian church with the name of Berhane Selassie.

In July 1977 Marley found a wound in his right big toe, which he blamed on a football injury. During a subsequent football match, he lost the nail but due to his religious beliefs he refused to have the toe amputated, despite medical advice that the problem was due to a skin melanoma.

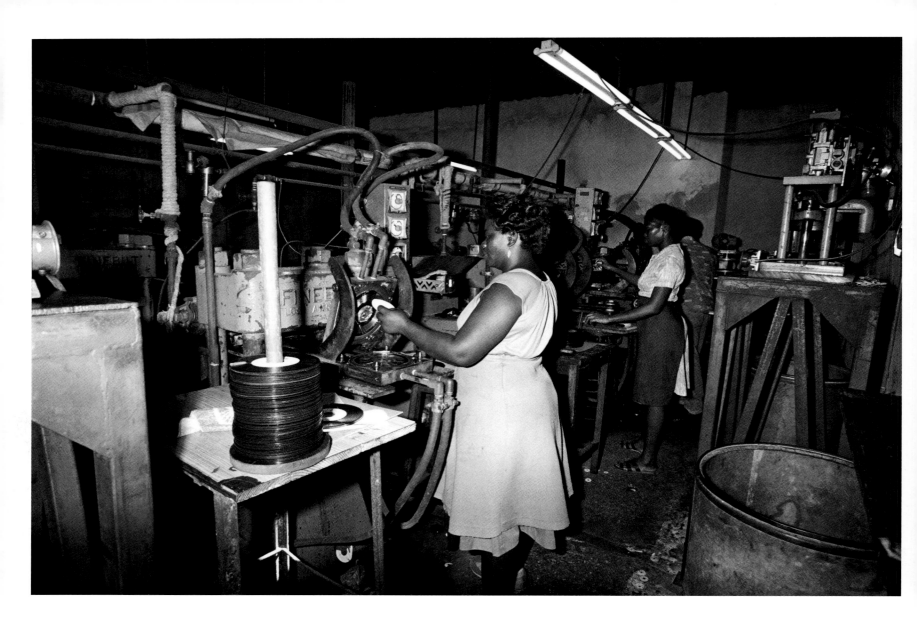

244 AND 245 [KINGSTON] - Two images of Bob Marley's Jamaican record label in Kingston.

Later the cancer spread to his brain and his condition deteriorated during the summer of 1980, collapsing after a series of Madison Square Garden concerts subsequent to his triumphant European tour, which had included the San Siro venue in Milan. Marley traveled from the US to Munich, Germany, to see the specialist oncologist Josef Issels, but it was too late, and Marley asked to end his days in Jamaica. Sadly his condition was too serious for him to reach home, and his plane was forced to land in Miami, where he died on May 11, 1981.

He is buried in a crypt at Nine Miles, his home village. His premature death fed rumors of a plot against him and caused his legend to grow. On February 6. 2005, on what would have been his 60th birthday, Bob Marley's "earthday" was celebrated in Addis Ababa, Ethiopia. An enormous crowd gathered in his honor as the world observed.

246 AND 247 [LONDON 1980] - During his brief career, the Jamaican musician invented a new form of reggae interweaving rock, soul, blues and funk sounds, in a new musical language that is enjoyed worldwide.

248, 249 AND 250-251 [BOB MARLEY LIVE]
- The Jamaican musician in concert, Santa Monica, USA.

248, 249 Bob Marley & The Wailers

The Queen story, one of a ride to stellar success and of a legend that just won't die, is certainly worth telling. The fact that we're still talking about Queen so many years after the demise of the electrifying Freddie Mercury in 1991, and considering the world tour that Roger Taylor and Brian May undertook alongside "stand-in" Paul Rodgers, in 2005, means that the band certainly left some mark on worldwide pop music. And that it will continue to leave traces in the future.

All of Queen's band members are (or were, in the case of Freddie Mercury, who died of AIDS), extremely talented musicians. They were capable of producing beautiful, complex songs and even though Freddie Mercury, as vocalist and with his outlandish personality, was always the most famous of the group, the other three wrote many of Queen's most popular hits. For instance, Roger Taylor wrote "Radio Gaga," Brian May wrote "We Will Rock You," John Deacon wrote "Another One Bites The Dust." (No lightweight himself, Freddie Mercury wrote "We Are The Champions," "Innuendo," and "Bohemian Rhapsody," among others.)

During his life, Mercury was the fulcrum of this balancing act of bubbly musicians and composers, and he was, of course, the prima donna. So his wonderful solo album with a "real" prima donna, Montserrat Caballè, must have been a moment of purest joy for Mercury the actor.

THE UNBEATABLE "QUEEN" OF BRITISH ROCK

Queen

253 [QUEEN, 1984] ▲ Freddy Mercury: voice and leader of Queen, on stage during a concert in 1984.

255 [USA, 1978] - Queen live. The band's concerts were real happenings and Freddy Mercury's vocal range made the crowds wild.

256 AND 257 [FREDDY MERCURY] - An innovative and eccentric figure, whose music and acts aroused great admiration. A rare artist able to create a perfect fusion of his two great passions: rock and opera.

Over-the-top concerts full of wild poses, plenty of operetta or skin-house trash, but also a great deal of theatrical play-acting, presented filled-to-capacity stadiums, with scores of plebeian dreams, dreams that, inevitably and always, divided critics from the opinion of the worshipful crowds in each corner of the world. From their debut, the cloned heavy metal band – with Freddie Mercury, vocals and pianoforte, Brian May, guitar, John Deacon, electric bass, and Roger Taylor, drums – struggled to be convincing for the critics. Instead they sold albums and filled concert venues. It was the early Seventies when Queen released *Queen* (1973) and *Queen II* (1974), but it wasn't until *A Night at the Opera* (1975) and the incredible "Bohemian Rhapsody," that Queen became Queen. After that, their commercial success was unstoppable, and they achieved planetary popularity, indifferent to trends, genres, or styles. *Jazz* (1978) and *Innuendo* were panned by critics, records, but people all over the world, from Italy to Brazil, Japan to Australia, America to Russia, loved Queen whatever the case, without critical distinctions and academic sophisms. Freddie Mercury himself defined his music as watered-down pop, to be heard and cast aside, returning the debate to the simplicity of a vision tied to the pop nature of the band's music as art of the present, brilliant. and ephemeral. Regardless, adoring audiences packed stadiums and arenas, bought records, and drove singles to the top of the charts.

Freddie Mercury gave his last interview in 1991, just before his death, soon after the release of *Innuendo*, a modern, moving album, perhaps their absolute best: "I don't want to change the world. For me, happiness is the most important thing and if I'm happy then it shows in my work. In the end, all the mistakes and all the excuses are down to me. I like to feel that I'm just being my honest self and as far as I'm concerned I just want to pack in as much of life and fun, having a good time as much as I can in the years I have." It was a real testament, and coupled with the courageous, ironic videos he made for this last album, a touching testimony of his vitality and his fragility.

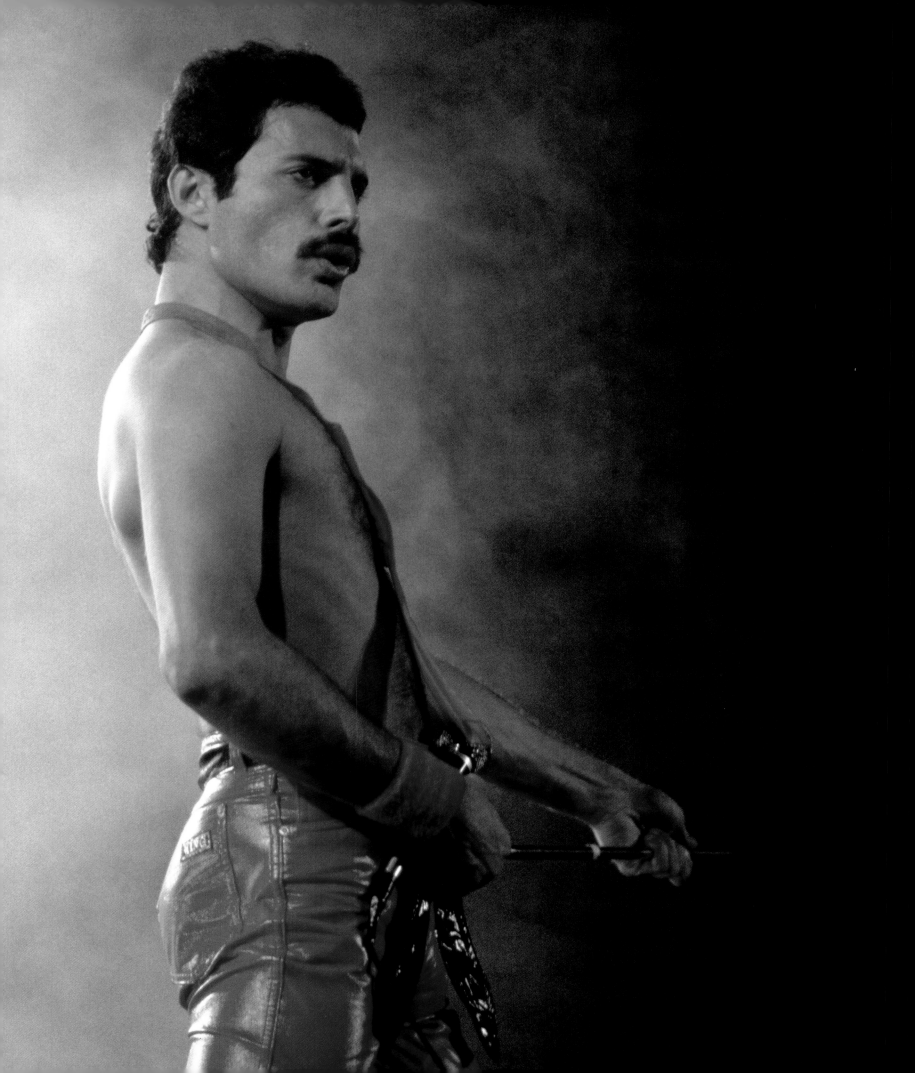

258 [PARIS, 1979] - Queen live in Paris. Following a long series of concerts, their first live album, "Live Killers", was released in 1979. ◄

259 [QUEEN] - The group line-up was John Deacon, bass, left, Freddie Mercury, vocals, Brian May, guitar and Roger Meddows-Taylor on drums.

260-261 ["QUEEN" OF THE STAGE] - Freddy Mercury immortalized in one of his costumes, during one of his last concerts, in 1986.

262 [LONDON, 1985] - Queen in Live Aid, London, organized to gather funds to help fight hunger in Africa.

Aerosmith are a Boston group, founded in 1972. Their role models were The Rolling Stones, and they shared the same

passion for the blues and for the street. The vocalist, Steven Tyler, is an American reincarnation of Mick Jagger and just like the

Brit star, plays a harmonica from time to time. The guitarist, Joe Perry, like Keith Richards, is the perfect foil for the vocalist, as

well as being the creator of some killer riffs. The Seventies albums are the best: outstanding *Get Your Wings* (Columbia, 1974),

Toys In The Attic (Columbia, 1975) and *Rocks* (Columbia, 1976), with the double *Live Bootleg* (Columbia, 1978).

They topped the charts with songs that combined rhythm 'n' blues with classic hard rock. After a less than brilliant

kickoff to their career, they managed to make progress thanks to the albums above, which show a very British influence in their

style (think Led Zeppelin meets The Rolling Stones) and started to convince growing masses of rock fans. To cut a long story

short, the group became huge and concerts were held in American football stadiums, just like other giants of rock. It was their

fantasy, but also the start of a deep crisis between Joe Perry and Steven Tyler, caused by a leadership crisis, possibly, or excessive

pressure, or too many hard drugs. A fate shared with all of the great Seventies rockers, heroin seemed always to be around

everyone, too often causing their deaths. The Aerosmith star was eclipsed (temporarily) in 1979, when Joe Perry and Brad

Whitford left the group. In 1982, Aerosmith tried again with two new guitarists, Jimmy Crespo and Rick Dufay, but the absence

of Perry and Whitford was conspicuous.

ROCK 'N' ROLL, GIRLS, SHEER ENERGY AND DREAMS FOR AMERICA'S "ROLLING STONES"

Aerosmith

266, 267 Aerosmith

265 [STEVEN TYLER] ⏶ The leader and vocalist of
the American rock band, Aerosmith, during a
performance at Washington Stadium, 2001.

266-267 [AEROSMITH, 1978] - The group early in their
career during taping of a special for NBC network
show.

So, in the interests of the group, which was fad-
ing away to nothing, the two reunited with Tyler and
the others, and celebrated their return with the
album *Done With Mirrors*, in 1985. Out of rehab and
ready to prove themselves again, they opened the
door to a rock-rap dialog, in the company of Run
DMC, the legendary founding fathers of the genre
that was to change the history of black music. "Walk
This Way" (a classic from the 1975 album *Toys In The
Attic*), re-recorded with Run DMC, was the seed
from which Aerosmith's new career blossomed,
thanks to the rap-rock fusion, and a marvelous video
that MTV aired in heavy rotation. Aerosmith were
on their way back to the top and seemed to be
touched by new inspiration. Albums like *Permanent
Vacation* (Geffen, 1987), *Pump* (Geffen, 1989), and
various anthologies that began to gather up their
discography, kept the group high in the charts.

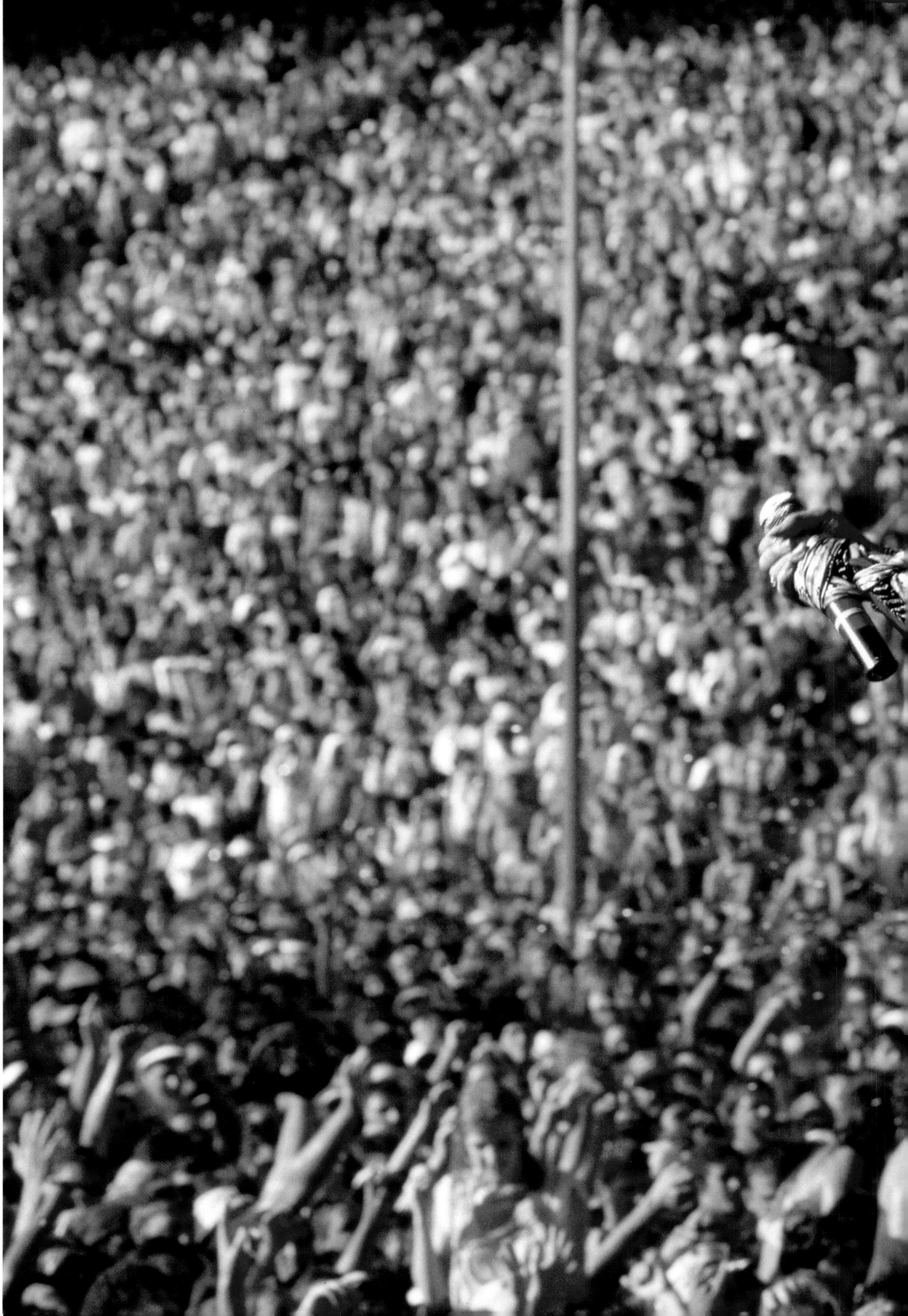

[USA, 1987] - Huge crowds during Aerosmith's 1987 tour.

270 [AEROSMITH IN CONCERT] - The band was formed after Joe Perry and Tom Hamilton met Steven Tyler; Joey Kramer (drums) and Ray Tabano (guitar) came later. In 1971 Brad Whitford replaced Ray Tabano.

271 [STEVE TYLER, 1986] - A short crisis in 1986 was soon followed by an upswing and a relaunch of the band. The track "Walk this Way," famous as one of the first rap/rock crossovers, was revived.

272 [WASHINGTON, 2001] - Aerosmith in a memorial concert for the victims of 9/11 (photo of Steve Tyler and Joe Perry).

273 [AEROSMITH AND KISS WORLD TOUR] - A Californian date for the world tour organized in 2003 by Aerosmith and Kiss.

They do boast a lengthy career and have entered the Rock 'n' Roll Hall Of Fame. Prior to their self-titled 1973 debut album they had built the band's foundations from scratch, playing in Boston clubs (one of their most famous pieces was a Fleetwood Mac cover, "Rattlesnake Shake," recorded during a Boston performance). Years later and throughout the Nineties, for lack of other great "classic" rock icons as bright as Aerosmith, they were obliged never to put a foot wrong – but they seemed to manage that well. They still play the blues, Tyler still plays his harmonica – as heard on *Honkin' On Bobo* (Columbia, 2004) – and time seems to have stood still for them. Aerosmith won't die: like The Stones, they must have a decrepit painting hidden in some attic.

274-275 [STEVEN TYLER] -
Thanks to the histrionic
leader and their hard
rock revival style,
Aerosmith became one of
America's and the world's
most popular bands.

When mid-Seventies color rock magazines began to circulate photos from the concerts of a New York group called Kiss, people couldn't believe their eyes. The logo looming behind the group on stage was a double Nazi "S", and it was on their record covers too. During concerts the bass player dressed as a vampire, spewing blood, and close-ups of this grotesque, unthinkable scene shocked the public and raised a storm. Kiss had landed on Planet Rock and they were there to stay. Their journey continues and many of those who criticized them were forced to give in to the evidence of a group that gained ground, fans and gold records, concert after concert, and record after record.

Kiss used some mysterious, yet effective, marketing ploys. The band never believed in the ideologies suggested by their logo, which they used simply for provocation and stage effect. The idea of arousing shock and dismay from theatrical effects came from a fusion of trash culture, horror B-movies, and that combination of excess and vulgarity that is no novelty on the rock stage. Or at least it wasn't in those days. Another gimmick that caused a commotion was the issue of their identity: from the start, the band hid behind face paint and meticulously got rid of any unmasked images. The fan club sent photos of the musicians without their make-up to new members, but the photos dissolved as soon as the envelope was opened (this may be an urban legend).

Kiss began in 1972, in New York when Wicked Lester, the group that Paul Stanley (rhythm guitar) and Gene Simmons

THE GREAT

(bass) were in together broke up. They were joined by Peter Criss (drums) and Ace Frehley (solo guitar).

ROCK'N'ROLL

CIRCUS

277 [PAUL STANLEY] ▲ Guitarist Paul Stanley, in the photo, and bass-player Gene Simmons, founded the group in 1972.

278 [KISS, 1976] - The group in concert early in their career. In 1976 they released the album "Destroyer," with its quintessential hard rock sound.

279 [KISS, 1979] - At the peak of their commercial and record success, Kiss exploited their image and popularity to market merchandise also.

The first three albums (1973's *Kiss* and *Hotter Than Hell*, and 1974's *Dressed To Kill*) weren't particularly successful, but the group built up a huge following of fans thanks to their pyrotechnical tour and macabre look. Each of the four had a costume and an identity. The focus of the show was the Vampire (aka Gene Simmons) and his extremely long tongue, spitting blood, breathing fire and playing a hatchet-shaped bass. A rock circus of flying musicians, explosions and ridiculously high volume that owed everything to Alice Cooper, but that initiated Marvel Comics-style America into the world of rock. The public were ecstatic and the double live album *Alive!* became an international hit, exposing the group's musical and instrumental talents, which were best expressed in the concert milieu. Songs like "Black Diamond" were pure rock storms in the tradition of other American bands like Steppenwolf, and worthy of their biggest contemporary rivals, the more refined Blue Oyster Cult.

In 1976 *Destroyer* was a huge hit, followed by *Rock and Roll Over*. In 1977 they released Love Gun, and in 1979 Dynasty, which contained the worldwide smash "I Was Made For Loving You," which allowed them to penetrate the great pop audiences. It was a dance number that rode the period's new electronic wave. From that time on, the group threw away their masks and the lineup revealed their true faces without stage makeup. In the Eighties and Nineties the band underwent a number of fast lineup changes, with the two founding members, Simmons and Stanley, remaining with the group, even today.

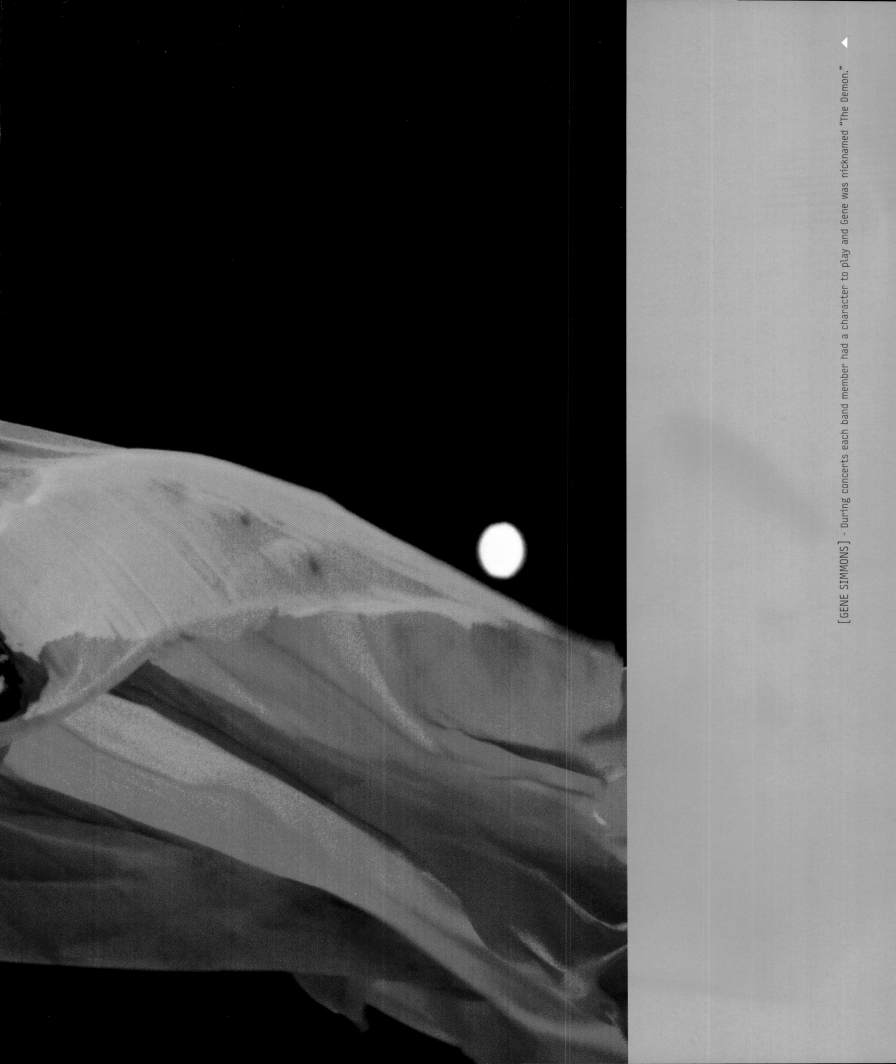

[GENE SIMMONS] - During concerts each band member had a character to play and Gene was nicknamed "The Demon."

284 AND 285 [CONNECTICUT, 2003] - Two images of Paul Stanley during the 2003 world tour organized by Aerosmith and Kiss.

1. Paul Stanley in "The Starchild" costume during the "Rock the Nation Tour," 2004.

2. Gene Simmons performing as "The Demon" at the Continental Airlines Arena in 2000.

3. and 4. Two images of Gene Simmons, the first in California in 2004 and the other during the 2003 Aerosmith and Kiss World Tour.

The band made its debut in a social center for the jobless, on November 6, 1975. After they'd been playing for ten minutes, the club managers shut off the electricity. The impact made by Johnny Rotten, Glen Matlock, Paul Cook, and Steve Jones was a bit too much for the time. The band had formed just a few weeks earlier in the alternative boutique Sex owned by Malcom McLaren, who wanted a rock band to promote the name of his business. He convinced four youths who hung around his boutique and the King's Road rock underworld of dropouts, who were fanatical about music but disgusted by rock-star glitter, to form band and live out his anarchical artistic philosophy. Things worked out well, because his plans encountered the iconoclastic fury of John Lydon (renamed Johnny Rotten) and Steve Jones' anti-rock rage. The pair immediately began to write very basic but very aggressive songs, as The Ramones were doing on the other side of the ocean in New York. An enormous psychic bridge was erected between The Ramones and The Sex Pistols on either side of the Atlantic: this was the reaction that spawned punk rock.

By the summer of 1976, The Sex Pistols were so famous on the underground circuit that the record companies could no longer ignore their existence. Their performances continued to provoke. Their concerts inspired other groups, including The Clash, Siouxsie and The Banshees, X-Ray Specs, The Buzzcocks, The Jam, and countless others, and their destructive musical action wiped out an entire generation of musicians in one fell swoop. Suddenly the rock scene woke up to the fact that it had aged and that the kids had new heroes.

THE PIONEERS
OF THE PUNK
REVOLUTION

Sex Pistols

In November 1976, EMI beat out Polydor and signed up The Sex Pistols to a £40,000 contract. In December they released their first single, "Anarchy In The UK," whose lyrics and music were in line with Malcom McLaren's situationist/anarchist theories and the rabid frustration of the white dropout Johnny Rotten. The song entered the charts. With lyrics that pointed a finger at the government and sent out negative messages to youth, declaring that there was no future in the UK and that he, Rotten, was the antichrist come to bring chaos, the song was an enormous problem for British censors and press. An incident on UK TV (five minutes into an interview with the Sex Pistols, a journalist was driven away by a flood of insults and swearwords) meant that the band's nationwide tour was canceled, EMI took "Anarchy In The UK" off the market and terminated the contract.

In March 1977, while the band was at the center of furious debate, Glen Matlock left and a friend of Johnny Rotten joined the band as bass player: his name was Sid Vicious. A&M terminated a £150,000 contract after a week, sacking the band for "misconduct," but that didn't scare off Virgin, who signed them up in May to record a long-awaited album. Meanwhile, the second single, "God Save The Queen" was released, attacking the monarchy exactly when Queen Elizabeth II was celebrating her Silver Jubilee, with some heavy lyrics: "God Save The Queen/The fascist regime." The record was wiped off every playlist but it still managed to top the charts and become the symbol of the punk revolt in the summer of 1977, the year when the entire European youth movement was shaken by revolutionary reawakenings, with punk rock playing quite a major role.

289 [BILL GRUNDY SHOW, 1976] An interview for the Bill Grundy Show caught the public eye after it ended in swearing and bad language.

290 [USA TOUR] - The line-up was vocalist Johnny Rotten, guitarist Steve Jones, drummer Paul Cook and bass-player Glen Matlock, who was later replaced by Sid Vicious.

291 [JOHNNY ROTTEN] - Two images of the Sex Pistols vocalist during two concerts.

[BUCKINGHAM PALACE, 1977] - 10 March 1977, in a ceremony outside Buckingham Palace, the group signed a contract with A&M Records. ◄

294-295 [JOHNNY ROTTEN] - The Sex Pistols vocalist during a concert in Dallas, USA.

296 [SID VICIUS AND JOHNNY ROTTEN] - In February 1977 Sid Vicious, formerly drummer with Siouxsie and the Banshees and The Flowers of Romance, replaced Glen Matlock on bass.

297 [JOHNNY ROTTEN] ♪ A close-up of Sex Pistols vocalist, Johnny Rotten, in a USA concert, 1978.

The release of *Never Mind The Bollocks, Here's The Sex Pistols* unleashed Pistols mania, with the nihilist Sid Vicious, embodiment of the "rock star looking to die" figure, and the smarter, elusive, and ironic Johnny Rotten in the spotlight. A poorly-planned American tour had them playing in unfavorable venues to hostile crowds in the southern United States; in Nashville and Austin concerts were broken up by the police. On the other hand, in America the Pistols were immediately swallowed as the latest European rock folly and they were soon a source of curiosity for the tabloid press on both sides of the Ocean. This underestimation of their stature irritated Rotten immensely and he was soon on a collision course with McLaren, deciding to split up the group in January 1978, quitting at the end of a concert in San Francisco. The situation within the group, with Vicious suffering serious psychological and heroin problems, was the last straw. Rotten went back to being Lydon in 1979 and created Public Image Ltd. Vicious, living in New York, killed his girlfriend Nancy Spungen and died of a heroin overdose himself, while awaiting trial on February 2, 1979. The Sex Pistols seemed to have been an extreme adventure that got out of hand.

"Jesus died for somebody's sins, but not mine." Her poisonous, supercilious introductory statement: a couldn't-care-less and sibylline declaration of war, in the snake-like style The Stones used in "Sympathy for the Devil," which begins with the formal, sarcastic "Please allow me to introduce myself" pronounced by Satan in person. Patti Smith fully intended to grab the crown slowly slipping off The Stones' head, which neither Iggy Pop nor Lou Reed had succeeded in gripping tightly enough. The only pretender, Patti Smith told William Burroughs in 1979, was Bowie, but he wasn't American.

In 1975, Patti Smith, believed she alone knew what rock 'n' roll was, and she felt she had to do something, shake people up, intervene. The shadow of that messianic and mediumistic spirit lingered over the subsequent runaway four years, until her retirement in 1979. This evolution – the call, the appearance, the preaching, the incredible following she acquired so fast but transformed into rejection, then her withdrawal from public view in disgust and breakdown – had something biblical, religious, even evangelical about it. Patti Smith is a well-educated American woman, she knows the Bible and French poets, but mainly she is steeped in rock 'n' roll: that's her real culture. It's a physical culture rooted in running away from home and beginning sexual exploration, rock concerts and sleepless nights, drugs and poetry, streets and cellars, guitars and dreams.

WHEN ROCK MEETS POETRY

Patti Smith

299 [THE POETESS] ▲ A 1977 portrait of punk singer and poet, Patti Smith.

300 [HOLLYWOOD, 1979] - Poetry and punk music from the album "Easter," during the concert at the Hollywood Palladium.

Patti Smith's rock initiation was when she saw The Rolling Stones for the first time, as a child, on *The Ed Sullivan Show*. She described the episode in 1973, in these terms: "They put the touch on me. I was blushing jelly. This was no mama's-boy music. It was alchemical. I couldn't fathom the recipe but I was ready. Blind love for my father was the first thing I sacrificed to Mick Jagger." Rock 'n' roll struck her hard, and the first effect, the disintegration of family ties, was the consequence. On the other hand, rock was calling, and adventure and freedom could be had only on the road. That's why rock was born in America, and why it's an essentially American culture, precisely because it responds to that sense of uprooting that is perceived so clearly only by roaming Americans, always marching towards some frontier they never reach.

Before she loved The Stones, Patti Lee Smith, from Pitman, New Jersey, loved Little Richard and The Ronettes, a vocal group whose songs she always included on stage even at the height of her career. At 18 she moved to New York: it was 1967 and the city was buzzing. Rock was youth culture, the poetic renaissance going down in San Francisco was tightly intertwined with the transgressive rock of Frank Zappa's Mothers, and the Grateful Dead's and Jefferson Airplane's trip-rock, while New York was under the spell of Dylan's poetry and Velvet Underground's experimentations, led by the post-industrial genius of Andy Warhol. Smith went to the lion's den, the Chelsea Hotel on 23rd Street, and struck up a friendship with avant-garde photographer Robert Mapplethorpe, who shared his room with her, becoming thereafter her official photographer for her album covers, including the last one, *Dream of Life*.

In October 1978, the same hotel was the scene of the tragic death of Nancy Spungen, stabbed by Sid Vicious, who died shortly after, in early 1979. When Patti Smith lived at the Chelsea, it was the hotel where rock groups stayed in New York. Patti watched and took it all in. In late 1970, she went to Paris, poetizing, admiring, and distorting her first love, Arthur Rimbaud. The cocktail being shaken was about to explode.

From her Chelsea Hotel observatory, Patti Smith watched rock culture live, and she wrote about it for *Creem* and *Rolling Stone*. She also published a volume of poetry, **Seventh Heaven**, and began poetry readings at St Mark's Church in lower Manhattan. Soon her friend, the rock critic Lenny Kaye, began to accompany her singing on guitar. This fusion of rock and poetry was the spark. From that moment, The Patti Smith Group took shape with increasing decision: she was joined by Ivan Kral, a stateless Czech refugee from Prague who played guitar, and Jay Daugherty on drums. Richard Sohl, who played piano, had been working for a while with Lenny Kaye during the poetry readings. They went to Island Records with "Piss Factory" and they were signed up. Word of the "rock poetess" was reaching Europe.

The band's performances at the CBGB, a Bowery rock club, and at Max's Kansas City some thirty blocks north, had spread the cult, and Arista hurried to snatch up the band. The rest is history: Patti Smith influenced the punk movement, becoming a great rock star, she went on to preach her beliefs on the rock stages of the world, until she gradually came to the realization that rock was not paradise, but hell, it was corrupt, money-grubbing, and impure like the rest of the world. Rock was not going to improve the world, only exploit it to hoard dollars. Then Patti pursued her love dream. Car, supermarket, a husband (Fred "Sonic" Smith, legendary member of MC5, from Detroit, the city where the Smiths settled), two sons, Jackson and Jessie, the problems of daily routine were Patti Smith's for nine long years. Then, the awakening, the comeback: *Dream of Life*. Since then she has been a discreet, alert presence in rock culture, without the former uproar and excess, but equally fascinating and mysterious, and still blending rock, poetry, spirituality, and hope.

302 [ROCK GARDEN, LONDON, 1978] - Patti Smith, dubbed the "damned priestess" of rock for her decadent poetry, political commitments and music.

302-303 [IN THE CROWDS, 1970] - Rock singer Patti Smith at the edge of the stage, kneeling in front of her audience, during a concert in 1970.

304 [NEW YORK, 1976] - The American singer during Saturday Night Live, New York.

305 [THE BEGINNINGS] - An image of Patti Smith from 1976, early in her career.

306-307 [APRIL 1978] - The 1978 ballade "Because The Night" (penned by Bruce Springsteen) became the driving track for the album "Easter" (1978).

308 AND 309 [PATTI
SMITH AND THE BAND] –
Patti Smith's band was:
Lenny Kaye, Bruce Brody, Jay
Dee Daugherty, Ivan Kral.

310 AND 311 [POLITICAL COMMITMENT] - Patty Smith in front of antifascist graffiti (first photo) and in military clothing (second photo).

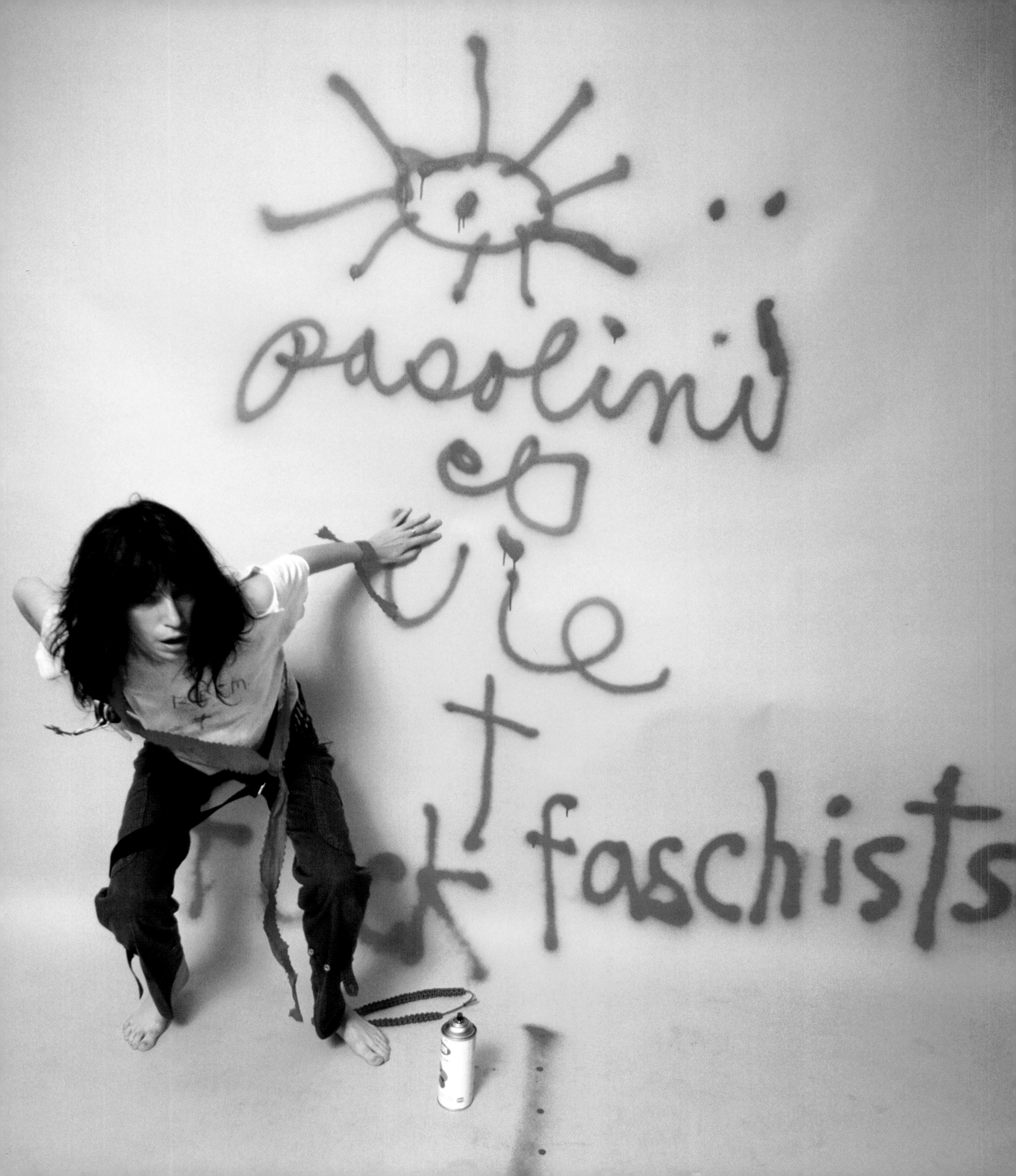
pasolini
faschists

In September 1974 Chris Frantz arrived in New York with his girlfriend Tina Weymouth, and joined forces with their college friend David Byrne to look for a loft to play in and develop their music. A rundown location turned up, in a deserted building, which was ideal, as they could play without bothering anyone, often all night, since they worked during the day. When the time came to choose a name, a friend suggested Talking Heads, the title of a TV show running in 1976. They decided it was awful enough to be a good name for a rock band, so Talking Heads they were. The band began playing at CBGB and as they improved, the audience grew, and so did their fame. They managed to get signed up by Seymour Stein at Sire Records, the record producer was Brian Eno. Jerry Harrison, who had been hanging around them for a while, joined the band full time. That, quite simply, was how a band formed that would go on to entrance millions of fans the world over. Even now that they have split up for good, with David Byrne keen to go his own way, audiences regret the passing of one of contemporary rock's most cutting-edge, creative groups.

Talking Heads really did break down barriers, right from the start. They were quite normal musicians, light years away **MUSIC, TECHNO** from the traditional rocker cliché, and the band just decided to explore all types of sounds and possibilities, **AND PASSION** without getting tied down to a priority culture.

Talking Heads

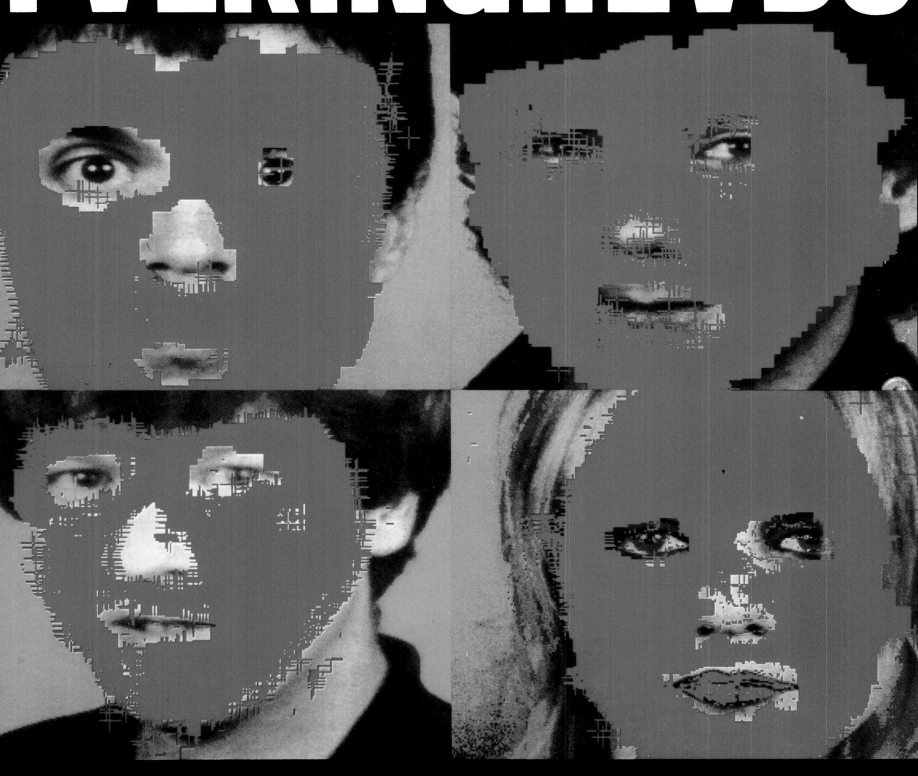

["REMAIN IN LIGHT"] - The cover of the fourth Talking Heads album "Remain in Light", released in 1980.

314 AND 315 [ROCK AND ROLL HALL OF FAME] - The Talking Heads playing at the Rock and Roll Hall of Fame, in New York's Waldorf-Astoria, 2002.

Talking Heads borrowed from James Brown soul and George Clinton funk right through to Third World cultures. They delved into world music, Marley's reggae, and were guided by accidental meetings, like that with Brian Eno, which enabled them to shake up the sleepy New York scene. The New Wave scene, bogged down by London-import trends, thanks to the band, was able to make a quality leap towards music without frontiers, without boundaries, without inferiority complexes.

Right from the start, David Byrne explained in 1992, he wanted his guitar sound to be thin and dry, metallic and clear, which is really the guitar's natural sound, not the violent, macho sound typical of rock. The guitar was going to speak its mother tongue, embedded in its nature as a contemporary instrument, the most contemporary of instruments, the most free of European aesthetics, the closest to African rhythms, the most American of instruments. Byrne was never able to bond with rock visions and he always hated drugs. Having tried some, the result was to reject them as they terrified him: they closed his mind, rather than opening it – they brought him darkness, not light. His compositions improved without the drugs and he was grateful that he didn't meet the same fate as many friends, musicians and non-musicians, whom he saw destroyed by chemical agents leading nowhere.

A clear stand and artistically at odds with the traditional picture of the ill-fated musician, yet essential for understanding just what was behind this creative volcano which started out with *Remain in Light* and reached *Sand in The Vaseline*, EMI's complete anthology, two CDs containing 33 tracks expressing the best of the band's existence, which lasted a decade, from the late Seventies to the mid-Eighties.

Describing the everyday struggles to survive in America, using the language of rock to give dramatic shape to the biographies of millions of common people battling with common problems, in an America that is often unjust and mean. Dealing head-on with important issues for American youth: racism, violence, peace, love, the American dream in tatters. This was Springsteen from the word go, in his legendary Stone Pony concerts at Asbury Park on the New Jersey coast. Narrator of every American's subconscious, to the point that he triggered contradictions in politics and in music: "Born In The USA" became so famous that Ronald Reagan used it to open his presidential campaign rallies in 1984, having misinterpreted the text as being a nationalist anthem, when it was actually a hard-hitting criticism of effects on Vietnam War veterans. Until that time, Bruce Springsteen had been known as a rock musician strongly influenced by two genres: folk and rock 'n' roll. *Born To Run*, the 1975 album that confirmed him as a star and got him on the covers of both *Time* and *Newsweek* in the same week (October 27), also made him known the world over as

THE LAST

the preacher of a restless America, full of young people suffering an identity crisis, and seeking profound values,

GREAT ROCK

undecided between integration and escape.

HERO

Bruce Springsteen

317 [BRUCE SPRINGSTEEN] ▲ Bruce Springsteen's music is rooted in American popular and folk music.

318 [BORN IN THE U.S.A.] - In the 1980s Springsteen confirmed his success with "Born In The USA." His popularity went beyond American borders.

319 [LONDON, 1985] - "The Boss" (as Springsteen is known) packed out Wembley Stadium, in London for a 1985 concert.

Bruce Frederick Joseph Springsteen was born on September 23, 1949, in Long Branch, New Jersey. His father was of Irish origin and his mother came from an Italian family. He decided to become a musician in 1956 after watching Elvis Presley on *The Ed Sullivan Show*. At 13 he bought his first electric guitar for 18 dollars, and in 1965 he was befriended by a local couple, Tex and Marion Vinyard, who helped young groups: with their support he founded The Castyles and recorded two songs in a public studio at Bricktown, New Jersey, then he started approaching New York clubs, including the famous Café Wha?, in Greenwich Village, where the as-yet unknown Jimi Hendrix was playing. Since then, he has played countless concerts, all never-ending and overwhelming, in giant stadiums (ten consecutive nights in 1999 at New York's Madison Square Garden, with the E Street Band, and three at the Shea Stadium in 2003, for *The Rising*, the record inspired largely by his reaction to the 9/11 attacks on the World Trade Center, to mention just the most recent), in which audience and musicians came together in a spiritual and physical union, full of moments of deep introspection and emotional drama, folk ballads shadowing Dylan and American dreams rolling on endless highways. Springsteen rock is now a classic.

[LONDON, 1985] - Springsteen on stage gives his all for his audience.

322 [CLARENCE CLEMONS AND SPRINGSTEEN] - The famous sax-player is part of the E Street Band, with Springsteen.

323 [E STREET BAND] - Springsteen with his group (Garry W. Tallent, Clarence Clemons, and Nils Lofgren).

324 AND 325 [USA, 1985] - The Boss's concerts are a concentrate of energy and vitality. Springsteen offers his fans hours of music and countless encores.

326-327 [LIVE] - An eloquent shot of Bruce Springsteen lying on stage during a concert, 1990s.

THE "DIVA" OF

MODERN POP

Total USA sales 61 million (worldwide 250 million copies)

Only Barbra Streisand has sold more in the USA (72 million)

Her albums have sold as shown:

1983 – *Madonna* 5 million (worldwide - 9 million).

1984 – *Like A Virgin* 10 million (worldwide - 19 million)

1986 – *True Blue* 8 million (worldwide - 21 million)

1987 – *You Can Dance* 1 million (worldwide - 6 million)

1987 – *Who's That Girl?* 1 million (worldwide - 5 million)

1989 – *Like A Prayer* 4 million (worldwide - 13 million)

1990 – *I'm Breathless* 2 million (worldwide - 6 million)

1990 – *Immaculate* 10 million (worldwide - 23 million)

1992 – *Erotica* 2 million (worldwide - 5 million)

1994 – *Bedtime Stories* 2 million (worldwide - 7 million)

1995 – *Something To Remember* 3 million (worldwide - 8 million)

1996 – *Evita* 5 million (worldwide - 11 million)

1998 – *Ray Of Light* 4 million (worldwide - 17 million)

2000 – *Music* 3 million (worldwide - 15 million)

2001 – *Greatest Hits Volume II* 1 million (worldwide - 7 million)

2003 – *American Life* 1 million (worldwide - 5 million)

2004 - *Re-invention Tour* (worldwide - 120 million)

2006 - *Confessions Tour* (worldwide - 195 million)

Madonna

The *Guinness Book of World Records* states that Madonna is the world's most successful female music artist. Warner Bros. Records states that Madonna has sold more than 250 million discs (75 million singles and 175 million albums), more than any other female artist. Madonna has had 12 number one singles in *Billboard's* Hot 100 Singles Chart, equal to Diana Ross and The Supremes and second only to Mariah Carey's 15, for female chart-toppers. Madonna has had six singles at number two in *Billboard's* Hot 100 Singles Chart, the highest of any woman and equal to Elvis Presley.

Madonna is certified by the Recording Industry Association of America (RIAA), as having 24 gold discs, four platinum, and one multi-platinum disc. She has sold 15 million singles in the USA, the highest number of any female artist. She has had five number one and five number two albums in *Billboard's* Top 200 Albums chart, ranked third after The Beatles' six and Frank Sinatra's seven.

Every one of Madonna's albums has ranked in the USA's top ten charts, except for *You Can Dance* and *Remixed & Revisited*. All albums released by Madonna in Great Britain have found their way into the top ten charts and her only album that didn't make it to the top five was her 1983 debut release.

330 ["DIE ANOTHER DAY"]   Madonna during shooting of the video for "Die Another Day," part of the soundtrack for the 2002 James Bond film.

332-333 [VIRGIN TOUR] - Madonna dancing on stage during the Virgin Tour, 1985. Her second album, "Like a Virgin," was a planetary hit.

▲ 1

▲ 2

1. Madonna on the 1987 "Who's That Girl Tour," performing in Atlanta.

2. Madonna singing during the "Girlie Show" tour, London, 1993.

334, 335 Madonna

▲ 3

▲ 4

3. "Girlie Show" tour, 1993.

4. Another world tour for Madonna: "Blond Ambition Tour," Japan in 1990.

336 AND 337 [CONFESSIONS TOUR, 2006] - Two images from the world tour "Confessions" at the American Airlines Arena, Miami, Florida (left), and Rome's Olympic Stadium (above).

Madonna is the world's most successful dance music artist, with 33 singles topping the *Billboard* Hot Dance/Club Play Single Chart, more than double the number achieved by Janet Jackson. She also has had 25 number one singles, three times the number achieved by her rivals Michael Jackson, Janet Jackson, Prince, and Notorious B.I.G.

Madonna has sold 14.6 million singles in the UK, more than any other female artist. From the *Evita* soundtrack in 1996, to 2000's *Music* album, Madonna had three consecutive number one album hits in the UK, a record unbeaten by any other female artist. In the UK, only Madonna and Kylie Minogue have had a number one album and a number one single in three different decades. The album *Immaculate Collection* was the biggest-selling female greatest hits worldwide, with over 23 million copies sold.

Madonna's videos are played more frequently than those of any other artist on MTV and she was voted the biggest video artist by MTV viewers in the 25 Greatest Video Stars chart. She was also voted the sexiest artist in the world, in VH1's 100 Sexiest Artists. Madonna has achieved more success than any other artist in the history of the MTV Video Music Awards, with 67 VMA Nominations and 19 wins.

In 2004 Madonna was one of the five founding members of the UK Music Hall of Fame, alongside Elvis Presley, The Beatles, Bob Marley, and U2 as artists taking their rightful place there.

Maverick Records was the most successful label ever run by a musician. While it was still being managed by Madonna (who had a 40 percent shareholding, with 60 percent held by Warner Bros., up to 2004), the company generated $1.2 billion. Madonna is the world's richest female artist, with an estimated estate in excess of $387 million, according to The Sunday *Times*, in April 2004. In February 2005, her fortune was estimated to be $441 million according to *Rolling Stone* magazine. In 2004, she earned another $54 million from her tour and record sales alone. Forbes reckon her to be worth about $600 million (2007) and the Re-invention tour took $120 million. The 2006 Confession Tour broke that record, cashing in $195 million.

If success is what counts in the culture industry, there's little doubt that Madonna has had more than her fair share in her more than 20-year career. And she isn't finished yet.

[NEW YORK, 2006] - Madonna in concert at Madison Square Garden, 2006.

[DÜSSELDORF, 2006] - The Confessions Tour 2006 also went to Germany. In the background, one of Madonna's most recent videos.

Michael Joseph Jackson (born August 29, 1958, in Gary, Indiana) is an American singer, record producer

and songwriter, who began his career as Jackson 5 vocalist at Motown Records in the Sixties and Seventies.

In 1979 he went solo and since then he has become the most successful African-American

musician in the history of music, and is popular worldwide. He is also known as the King of Pop. During his

career he has garnered legions of devoted fans, but his success has also triggered an identity crisis caused by

his own media image, that has made him seek to change his appearance and to live as a recluse. He loves

children and apart from his large donations to charities, he has also dedicated special areas at Neverland, his

ranch, where he invites disadvantaged children to visit. Unfortunately, precisely this involvement led to his

"THE KING OF POP"

being accused of indecent acts towards minors, like the most infamous case in May 2005, in Santa Maria,

FROM DREAMS

California, of which he was acquitted.

TO DUST

Michael Jackson

343 [JACKSON LIVE] ▲ The American singer in concert in 1984 to promote the album "Victory."

345 [SINGAPORE, 1993] - Michael Jackson in the first of two concerts at the National Stadium, 1993.

346 [MICHAEL AND ANDY WARHOL] - International pop icon Michael Jackson being painted by American artist, Andy Warhol.

347 [PORTRAIT, 1984] - In 1984 a shower of awards for "Thriller" and for the "E.T. Storybook" (eight Grammies altogether).

Jackson has received numerous awards from the music industry, including 18 Grammys, and is estimated to have sold from 200 to 300 million copies of his records worldwide. His video for "Thriller" is considered an all-time music video great and a huge step forward in the artistic acknowledgment of pop videos. MTV and *Rolling Stone* magazine recently elected four of his songs as among the top 100 pop songs ever written. In descending order: "Billie Jean" at number five, "I Want You Back" with The Jackson 5 at number nine, "Beat It" at number 23, and "Rock with You" at number 82. His album *Thriller* is the top-selling album in history, in excess of 50 million copies (as of 2003) and in the US it is also the best-selling record of those containing only origi-nal music (26 million copies to date, second only to The Eagles' *Their Greatest Hits* 1971-1975, which 28 million copies to date). Seven singles that entered the Billboard Top 10 were taken from *Thriller*, released in 1982. The video of "Billie Jean," from *Thriller* was the first video by a black artist to be shown on MTV, and the mini film "Thriller," included in "The Making of Michael Jackson's 'Thriller'," became the most popular home video sold worldwide at that time. The three videos "Billie Jean," "Thriller," and "Beat It" are still amongst the videos enjoying biggest airplay in MTV and MTV2 playlists, and on VH1 television.

While performing "Billie Jean" during the TV special "Motown 25: Yesterday, Today, Forever," on the evening of May 16, 1983, Michael Jackson danced his famous moon-walk step for the first time, leaving viewers astonished. In January 1984, at the American Music Awards, Jackson was nominated for nine awards, winning eight, a record equaled only by Whitney Houston for the 1994 *The Bodyguard* soundtrack.

Inspired by the UK's Band Aid, Jackson was decisive in the conception and organization of the recording of the single "We Are the World" (which he wrote with Lionel Richie), in 1985, to gather funds for USA for Africa, a charity set up to help the starving in Africa. "We Are the World" was sung by 44 different artists including Harry Belafonte, Cyndi Lauper, Diana Ross, Ray Charles, and Stevie Wonder. The record sold seven million copies in the United States and was the biggest-selling single in the history of music, only later eclipsed by Elton John's 1997 version of "Candle In The Wind," a memorial for the late Princess Diana of Wales.

In 1986 Jackson starred in *Captain Eo*, a 3-D movie produced by George Lucas and Francis Ford Coppola, screened only in Disney theme parks until 1998. Reported to have cost $17 million, the film was, minute for minute, the costliest movie ever produced in the history of cinema. The movie contained the songs "We Are Here To Change The World" and "Another Part Of Me."

In 1987 Jackson released *Bad* and began a world tour, playing to packed stadiums. The year after, he released a movie called *Moonwalker* and a very serious autobiography called *Moon Walk*.

Soon *Bad* became the world's second top-selling album, after *Thriller*.

The records listed are just a few: the list could go only for many more pages. Some whisper that Michael Jackson is an alien. How else could we explain his incredible list of successes?

1. Moonwalk. The vocalist on stage performing the dance that made him famous.

2. Michael Jackson, 1984. The singer performing again with the Jackson 5, in other words the five Jackson brothers (Jackie, Jermaine, Tito, Marlon and Michael).

2 ▸

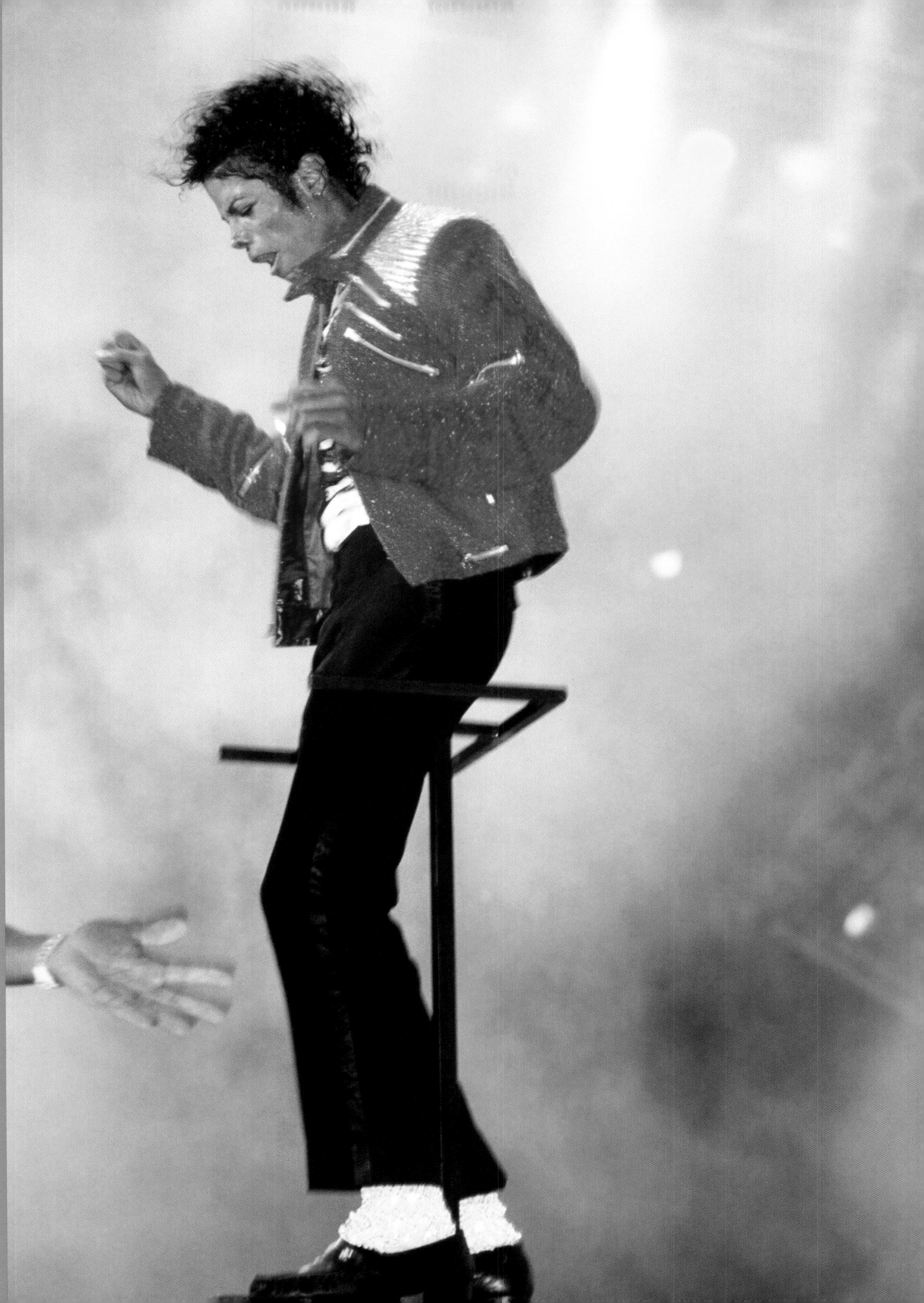

350 [VICTORY TOUR, 1984] - This tour was a huge success with fans: Michael was, by now, a massive musical phenomenon.

350-351 [BAD TOUR, 1988] - This was one of the biggest tours ever organized and the first series of concerts with Michael Jackson solo on stage.

352 AND 353 [BAD TOUR, 1988] - Two dates on the world tour for the album "Bad," released 31 August 1987, which went to number one in 24 countries.

Zooropa is quite different from *Boy*, the 1980 Bono and Co. debut. Only 13 years and yet how much inge-

nuity and lightheartedness there was then in *Boy*, what scant awareness of the world and the processes of com-

munication that U2 would interpret. Adolescent discs by groups just starting out, like the follow-up *October*,

reflecting daily, emotional problems. U2 were still linked to the New Wave world from which they started, and

the influence of the music they had encountered beforehand is easy to identify. Then, in 1983, something

clicked in the band, and with *War* they made the quality leap: U2's rock music became the "combat rock" pro-

claimed by The Clash. The album was mature, and cast Ireland as the symbol of wasted life because of racial and

religious madness. Emotion emerged from The Edge's addictive guitar riffs, the people of rock replied, acclaim-

ROCK

ing *U2 Rolling Stone*'s 1983 Band of The Year, and the album sold and sold and sold, beating all sorts of records.

CAN SAVE

THE WORLD

U2

355 [THE EDGE AND BONO] ▲ The Irish rock band performing at Live 8, July 2005.

357 [LONDON, 1985] - The first Live Aid concert at Wembley Stadium including countless rock stars. U2 gave one of the most touching performances, captivating the live audience but also the rest of the world, watching on cable.

358-359 [BONO IN CONCERT, 1986] - Paul David Hewson (stage name Bono Vox) vocalist and founder of the group during a concert: it was the time of the album "The Unforgettable Fire," recorded by U2 in magical Slave Castle.

After the live parenthesis of *Under A Blood Red Sky* came the masterpiece: Brian Eno entered the scene and in 1984 U2 generated *The Unforgettable Fire*; this album, paired with 1987's *The Joshua Tree*, forms U2's "magnum opus." *The Unforgettable Fire*, is a mystical record, based on its musical beauty and content. The band had discovered the great American continent: with *Fire* they explored the spiritual, ideal part; *Joshua Tree* sought out music and people's culture. They were on a two-leg journey: one symbolic, one real. They gathered a series of references that leave their traces even in subsequent work, in particular on *Rattle and Hum* (though this 1988 album and film and marked by confusion and too much provincial self-celebration). America is seen as an inexhaustible source of symbols and myths and as a giant mirror reflecting the terminal stage of European culture, and is explored by the new Irish emigrants, with naïve depth, resulting in a cultural tourism marking the new era of U2's music.

It was not until *Achtung Baby* in 1991 (produced by Daniel Lanois and Brian Eno), that the standard rose again: from reality to television hyper-reality, in the electronic agora where real becomes even realer, better, more desirable. The leap was noteworthy, the media debate undertaken through the media acquired new depths. *Achtung Baby*, possibly U2's profoundest and most desperate record, was an emotional storm of musical complexity that initially left the group's fans puzzled. The opus felt the fall of the Berlin Wall, a symbol the band adopted in the live show, and which seemed to have given them unexpected creative drive. The U2 of *Boy* and *October* was now lost in the mists of time.

This experiment culminated in the great Zoo Tour multi-communications project. With its retinue of video installations, and TV recordings, U2 used every possible register to manipulate music and make it a sort of "real" product of "reality." Their objective was to produce music that was readable and catchy as a direct derivation of worldwide events, perhaps unconsciously adhering to Dadaist automatic writing theories or the stream of consciousness developed by the American beat avant-garde after WWII. In any case, rock was just the last of the offspring of these literary currents, the most spurious and damned child, but the family tree exists and can't be hidden. U2 is proof of that.

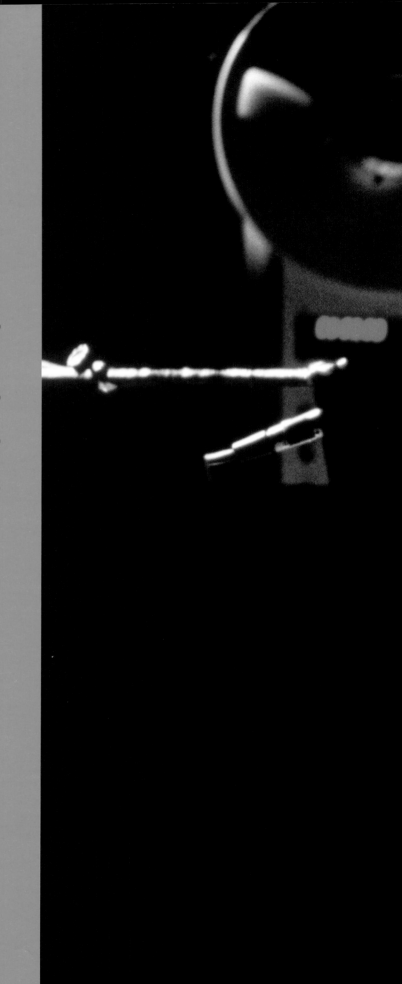

[NEW MEXICO, 1987] - The Edge, U2 's guitarist during the tour for the album "The Joshua Tree," Las Cruces.

362 [CALIFORNIA, 1997] - The album "POP," released in 1997, puzzled band fans with its "disco" sound; the promotional tour, generally known as the "Popmart Tour," was presented by the band in a store that was part of a large American supermarket chain.

363 [ADAM CLAYTON] - U2's guitarist performing at Oakland Stadium, California, in 1997.

364 AND 365 [PARIS, 1997] -
Two images of Bono Vox at
Parc des Prices (Paris),
during a concert hallmarked
by special effects and on a
stage designed by Willie
Williams, who also worked
on the Zoo TV tour. During
the concert a huge lemon
was hung over a LED screen
more than 145 feet in length.

366 [NEW YORK, 2004] - The Irish band during a free and impromptu concert at the Empire-Fulton Ferry Landing, under Brooklyn Bridge, New York.

367 [VERTIGO TOUR, 2005] - Bono Vox on stage at the Olympic Stadium in Berlin, a leg in the Vertigo Tour promoting the album "How to Dismantle an Atomic Bomb."

368-369 [SYDNEY, 2006] - The Edge, Larry Mullen Jr, Bono and Adam Clayton on stage at Sydney's Telstra Stadium during the fifth leg of the Vertigo Tour.

Behind the music of R.E.M. there is a secret concept, a sort of manifesto, a guiding light that has

always driven their creativity. It is englobed in a statement made by Peter Buck some years ago, during

an interview with a big American magazine. The concept is the underpinning to the vision behind the

band's entire artistic production and backlights not only their beginnings but also their most recent pro-

ductions. Peter Buck, co-founder of the group with Michael Stipe, in 1980, in Athens, Georgia, declared

that all forms of popular music were dead since they had been destroyed by mass communications.

When it's possible to buy anything from a hamburger to a favorite song, then you know it's really over.

THE NEW AMERICAN

Nevertheless, good artists can always revitalize any form of expression. It's a withering concept that

ROCK DREAM

Adorno would have subscribed to.

R.E.M.

In the early Eighties, R.E.M. felt that a world was dead and another was soon to emerge. Their contribution was writing music, composing songs, producing new popular music, synchronized with the seconds that they were living in their American observatory, the small college town of Athens, Georgia. They began with intimate, dreamy pictures ("Radio Free Europe," "Gardening at Night"), supported by beat tremors that sank their roots deep into the electric purity of psychedelic sounds borrowed from The Byrds, but that were nuanced by the years when they were produced. There was already a vein of pain and melancholy, but also positivity and strength. Not nostalgia, but an appeal to gather up energies for a leap still to be made. That leap which appeared clear in *Fables Of The Reconstruction*, the Athens quartet's first "revolutionary" record, in which violins and violoncellos, saxophones, trumpets, and folk instruments cloud and streak the band's beat harmonies. An infusion of contemporaneity in a rock language perceived, at this point, as repetitive and heading for closure. It is the implementation of the concept that Buck had always had in mind: if art is dead, then the good artist can resuscitate it. With this 1985 record, R.E.M. initiated the adult phase of their project. The teenage adventure of worldwide rock was over; it was time to begin mature management of the language they had perfected. The aesthetic project prevailed over the youthful ideal and the musical dream became a lifestyle: clear, realizable, concrete. The conscious experimentation with the creative flow got under way, and the clear, rational creation of music that really would be popular, therefore coherent with the time that spawned it. Each R.E.M. album that followed breathed the air of its period and became a sort of sound comment.

So what type of project is intertwined with R.E.M.'s notes? The two albums that start the Nineties, *Out of Time* (with "Losing My Religion," a worldwide success and their confirmation as "rock stars") and *Automatic For The People* are the most explicit. It is no coincidence that precisely with these two albums R.E.M. entered the category of million-disc bands. Nor was it a case of the classic emotional devaluation process that usually opens the gates of success. In fact, with R.E.M. the closure towards the public dimension increased inversely with the growth of their following and the diffusion of their name, which speaks clearly in favor of the group achieving the final stage of its artistic project. If the good artists revived a musical genre, then music can walk alone, live amongst the people, and the authors can stop intervening, step aside. After the release of *Automatic for the People*, R.E.M. didn't tour, or give interviews, they didn't show their faces at all. The music went ahead and they stepped back. These are the salient steps of their artistic biography, the only one that counts, really. There was no certainty that the R.E.M. project would be a success, at the beginning, contrasting as it did with current mass communication trends. The facts, however, showed things differently.

371 [MICHAEL STIPE] ▲ R.E.M.'s vocalist during a concert in the 2005 European tour to promote the album "Around The Sun".

373 [R.E.M., 1984] - The group was founded in 1980 by Michael Stipe (vocalist), Peter Buck, (guitarist) , Michael Edward Mills (bass-player) and William Thomas Berry (drummer, who left the band in 1997).

e.com

[LONDON, 2005] - REM during Live 8 London, Hyde Park.

They were the most influential group of the Eighties, at least in the early years, a group that marked a sharp musical turning point for rock. No one else had come up with any sound like it – or the mood or the music. Definitely a group that between 1978 and 1983 sold a million copies with just five albums (*Outlandos d'Amour*, 1978, *Reggatta de Blanc*, 1979, *Zenyatta Mondatta*, 1980, *Ghost in the Machine*, 1981, and *Synchronicity*, 1983) and collected dozens of gold and platinum discs, as well as millions of spectators. An impressive list of achievements for a trio in 1977 punk/New Wave London who were out to say what they thought, jumping on the rampant record industry bandwagon of those unique days. These were three veterans from different backgrounds. Not a rock trio at all – not even punks, as it happens, maybe we could call them pop, but with other nuances: jazz, reggae, and a range of other music. An explosive combination that soon ... exploded. In those days they were in close contact with the punk movement, as the office of their manager Miles Copeland was in the same building as the Sex Pistols' manager. On club nights they ended up playing before or after bands like The Damned: the pressure was high and The Police weren't especially welcome: too adult, too clean, not punk enough.

THE MESSAGE IN THIS BOTTLE: REGGAE'N'ROLL

Police

379 [POLICE, 1980] - A portrait of The Police, from the left: Andy Summers, Sting and Stewart Copeland.

380 [POLICE] - The three band members in a 1980s photo.

381 [LONDON, 1979] - Sting, Copeland and Summers playing on the Thames Embankment.

Sting (born Gordon Sumner), Stewart Copeland, and Henry Padovani had a tough time establishing themselves in 1977. The crucial moment was the arrival of Andy Summers, an accomplished and creative musician (he'd worked with Soft Machine, Deep Purple, Mike Oldfield, and Robert Fripp). Following the departure of Padovani, the trio decided to go beyond punk and exploit the rhythmic talent of Copeland and Sting's melodic abilities to give Summers the songs to which he could apply his magical arpeggios and delicate weaving, using flangers, echoes and delays with expert skill.

The base lines all became reggae, a style that few whites were exploiting, and Clapton's cover of "I Shot the Sheriff," six years earlier, was still memorable as an exception. Police's first album was a string of classics in the making: "Roxanne," "Can't Stand Losing You," "So Lonely," "Next To You." "Roxanne" got Police into the charts all over the world and the band left the dirty punk clubs of London for the great American and European stages. The second album, *Reggatta*, is the band's perfect album.

382 AND 383 [FAME, 1979] - The Police finally became famous in the UK and in Europe, releasing the single "Roxanne." 1979 was also the year of two long tours (see images).

A refined jazz technique bound Copeland and Summers, united by vast instrumental expertise and an ability to write simple, direct music, with immediate impact yet profound – as only great rock can be. All was running like clockwork: recording production, songs, performance.

1979 was their year, and also the year in which the trio finally shrugged off the punk shadows lingering from the first album. *Reggatta de Blanc* was a shared triumph, Summers' guitar reigning supreme in every song, meshing perfectly with Copeland's jazz-influenced percussion and Sting's wailing vocals. The all-time classic is "Message In A Bottle." for its magical arrangements and musical writing, as well as for the lyrics; it's a real rock gem. "It's Alright For You" has perfect drums (it's a Copeland song) and perfect guitar. "Bring On The Night" and "Walking On The Moon" send shivers down the spine with their rarified lyrical atmospheres, and splendid sound and music.

Then The Police began changing; the other three albums are excellent but less spontaneous. The arrangements are more thought out, articulated, electronic. It seems that the magic moment of their art had waned, although the trio were still putting together marvelous stuff (just look at "Every Breath You Take"). The band had three more years of success, but Sting started to lose interest, looking for other experiences, other outlets, other expressions. After 1983, the group decided to take time out and since then, the years have rolled past. They've never officially split up, but each member has gone his own way.

A long-awaited reunion was announced for 2007: a huge and wildly successful world tour. Obviously there is always need of this sort of Police.

384 AND 385 [STING ON STAGE] - Sting soon went for a solo career, with his first album "The Dream of the Blue Turtles" (1985), including the single "If You Love Somebody Set Them Free."

A bunch of dreamers making delicately electric, sinuously woven blues against a background of semi-acoustic musical horizons.

That's how they looked to the British scene when the streets of London were a turmoil of punk rockers chasing the Sex Pistols. They

had a precise agenda: they wanted to be heard on their own terms, which, ironically, was quite the opposite of what the London scene

had to say at that time. Dire Straits made it clear right away to the music world that they were different and unique.

Founded in 1977 by Mark Knopfler (guitar and vocalist), David Knopfler (guitar), John Illsley (bass), and Pick Withers (drums), at

a time when classic rock was in deep trouble following the punk rock revolution, Dire Straits had the guts to stick to their style and

come up with a different sound, blues and country. They were definitely in a time warp, and they stood out immediately.

Mark's voice was a rough whisper, an almost sloppy style that brought to mind Dylan. The stories they were telling sounded

like the real thing.

A GUITAR

Dire Straits released their first album in 1978, and their first single, "Sultans of Swing," in 1979. It went to number four in the US

ON THE ROAD

charts and number eight in the UK. It was an odd, magical rock song that described a jazz group, telling the rock kids in the dance hall

where the Sultans of Swing played that they didn't know anything about music. The portrait of a cultural gap, perhaps a snapshot of

a real situation the group's musicians had actually experienced. It was the first of the many refined screenplay-like sketches that Mark

Knopfler continued to compose for the next 10 years. There was "Lady Writer" (1979), "Romeo and Juliet" (1981), "Skateaway"

(1981), "Private Investigations" (1982), "Twisting By The Pool" (1983), "So Far Away" (1985), "Money for Nothing" (1985).

Dire Straits

387 [MARK KNOPFLER] ▲ The Dire Straits guitarist performing at San Francisco, California in 1979.

388 [DIRE STRAITS IN CONCERT, 1979] - The band was founded in 1977 by Mark Knopfler (guitar, voice and author of all songs), David Knopfler (guitar), John Illsley (bass) and Pick Withers (drums).

389 [LONDON, 1988] - Eric Clapton playing with Dire Straits during a concert organized to celebrate Nelson Mandela's 70th birthday.

Knopfler's themes were always anchored to reality and the quality of sound, lyrics and music built him a solid reputation as a guitarist. A shy, retiring musician, not part of the rock cliché, who stayed in the shadows on stage, almost dodging the lights, he was immediately spotted by the big stars like Dylan and Steely Dan, who asked him to guest on their records.

The second album, *Communiqué*, was released in 1979 and confirmed the expectations generated by the first release. The group continued to be successful, but Knopfler wanted more energy, to get his mindset out of the clubs and onto rock stages. He contacted a specialist for the third album, *Making Movies* (1980), inviting Roy Bittan (from Bruce Springsteen's E Street Band) to play keyboards. The album emerged with a greater articulation and widened the group's musical action to create a definite style that characterized Dire Straits production from then on: *Love Over Gold*, 1982, and chiefly the mega *Brothers in Arms*, 1985. This was a world success and was welcomed in the USA as an American record. In effect, it was just that, in its own way. On the cover the America dreamed by Knopfler echoed out of the shiny Dobro guitar, the quintessential Delta Blues instrument.

After that, the group cartwheeled at dizzy speed until Knopfler stepped on the brakes and began looking at other projects, dedicating himself to his beloved soundtracks. At the end of the day, Dire Straits was a big solo adventure, the musical mask used by the British guitarist. Yet another devotee of the Fender Stratocaster and its clean, dry sound who saw music as the mirror of life and soul.

In February 1984, at the height of their fame Duran Duran (The Fab Five) were honored with the cover of the rock

bible, *Rolling Stone* magazine. A British rock group couldn't have hoped for more. The history of *Rolling Stone* covers are a

sort of compendium of great rock, and getting to appear on one isn't the easiest thing in the world. Besides this, in 1982,

Diana, Princess of Wales, had said that Duran Duran were her favorite group and the British press nicknamed them the Fab

Five, paraphrasing the title enjoyed by The Beatles who were, of course, The Fab Four: another great honor.

The Duran Duran story began in 1978, when two high school mates, Nick Rhodes (keyboards) and John Taylor (bass),

formed a group in Birmingham (later they were joined by Roger Taylor, drums, Andy Taylor, guitar, and Simon Le Bon,

vocals) that successfully jelled the raw energy of The Sex Pistols with Chic's dance style, and the alternative elegance of

David Bowie and Roxy Music. The group was also influenced by other bands and singers, including Mick Ronson, The Clash,

BRIT POP

Japan, and New York's Blondie. Like Depeche Mode, Duran Duran were among the first groups to do their own remixes.

TAKES OVER

AMERICA

Duran Duran

392, 393 Duran Duran

391 [THE GROUP IS BORN] ▲ Duran Duran were founded in 1978 by Nick Rhodes and John Taylor; later the line-up grew with the arrival of Roger Taylor, Andy Taylor and Simon Le Bon.

392-393 [LOS ANGELES, 1993] - An image of Duran Duran taken in 1993, the year they released a second album called "Duran Duran" – but known as "The Wedding Album" to distinguish it from the first album of that name released 12 years earlier.

Before digital synthesizers and musical sampling were widespread, Duran Duran were already creating complex, multilayer arrangements for their singles, sometimes with performances that were surprisingly different from the original composition. Usually these "night versions" were available only on the flip side of vinyl 45s, until *Night Version: The Essential Duran Duran*, a 1998 compilation, was released.

From the word go, Duran Duran's style and music were hallmarked as elegant and clean in form and image. Not just refined, leading-edge equipment producing electronic sound and new "Eighties" mixes, but also stylists, names of the caliber of Perry Haines, Kahn & Bell, and Anthony Price were invited to implement an image strategy that would give the group that extra something to set them apart from the classic stereotype of the period's neo-romantic group look.

394 AND 395 [ANDY AND JOHN TAYLOR, 1984] - Two images from the long 1984 tour (Sing Blue Silver tour) following release of "Seven and The Ragged Tiger," which included successes like "Union of The Snake," "New Moon On Monday" and "The Reflex."

In 1985, after years of non-stop tours and studio sessions, Duran Duran decided it was time for a rest, a long rest away from the frenetic lifestyle they'd been living. What was meant to be time out turned into a disbanding. History was changing, Live Aid had shown the world a rock scene that had more to it than the manic nightclubbing and ludicrous fashion, which the British scene (with Duran Duran in pole position) somehow represented.

It's not uncommon, even now, for Duran Duran to be identified as the quintessential music group of the Eighties, despite the on-going evolution they showed over the years of their existence, with various lineups and breakups, followed by returns to the scene. They sold over 70 million records, with at least 80 singles getting into Billboard's Top 100 best-selling records, 30 in the UK's Top 40, including "Planet Earth," "Rio," "Hungry Like a Wolf," "Save a Prayer," "Is There Something I Should Know," "The Reflex" and the theme song for the James Bond movie "A View A Kill" in 1985. They continued in the Nineties with "Ordinary World" and "Come Undone," and have now conquered their third decade with "Sunrise" and "What Happens Tomorrow," found on the 2004 album *Astronaut*.

398-399 [SIMON LE BON, 1989] - During the 1980s the Duran Duran vocalist became extremely popular with teenagers of the time, because of his look and voice.

With the album *For You*, the diminutive Minneapolis genius known as Prince introduced himself to the world in 1978, after ten years slogging behind the scenes in his home city. It was most definitely an interesting debut, but he didn't make the big time. The artist's real milieu was on stage, where he performed wearing a garter belt and stockings, wearing heavy face makeup (a homage to greats like Little Richard and Rick James), but the shock turned to awe once he began paying the guitar. At that point, Jimi Hendrix became the icon he most resembled. Soul to funk via rock and punk was the route Prince took to success.

An accurate portrait of this musician, as Prince himself said, is of "a generation with new strength." We're right on Planet Prince here. Record after record, from his multi-platinum *Purple Rain* to *Sign O'The Times*, to the legendary *Black Album*, with its enormous homage to James Brown, and the more disjointed but nonetheless top-quality triple-album set *Emancipation*. Prince has played with Rick James, Morris Day and The Time; he's joined the legendary George Clinton

ROCK
on stage; he produced and album by Mavis Staples, already known to the rock public for her other collaborations (includ-

AND SOUL
ing Scorsese's movie *The Last Waltz* with The Band, Clapton, and others).

GET PURPLE

402 [PURPLE RAIN TOUR, 1984] - Prince rules the stage for the opening of his Purple Rain Tour in 1984.

403 [LIVE, 1986] - Prince lying flat on the stage during one of his 1986 concerts.

The bottom line is that Prince extended his circle and sought a consensus. Throughout his career, Prince has never hidden the fact that he longed to feel the comfort of being held in esteem by other musicians; he wanted to break his isolation and always find a reason to continue making music. The great success of the *Batman* soundtrack also highlighted Prince's weakness: the narrow gap that often stops him getting on the commercial carousel that Michael Jackson so easily rides. The grave is always just a step away, and Prince often walks on the edge: in this instance, he may well have briefly lost his footing. After *Batman*, however, he released *Graffiti Bridge* and the Minneapolis genius recovered his hold. The album is considered the peak of contemporary Prince production, and proved what we'd surmised all along: once his artistic and personal crises were resolved (hinted at by the sentence he speaks as the record opens, before the music, addressing his father and admitting that things sometimes hadn't gone the way he'd wanted, and that often something inside made him feel as if he was exploding), the musician undeniably filled his role as the chosen intermediary between historic funk and new urban rap, installing himself in a dimension between rock and soul and plunging both right and left, leaving himself plenty of room to maneuver.

404 [MIAMI, 2007] - Prince during a show at the Miami Convention Center during the Super Bowl.

405 [LOS ANGELES, 2006] - Prince takes the stage for the 36th NAACP Image Awards at the Dorothy Chandler Pavilion.

Electronics and sheer physical presence (like the hand snapping often heard between tracks), balanced by catchy and romantic with brash rhythm patterns, broken up by solitary music and sounds that sounded like they could have been made by just anybody out on the street in the black districts: *Graffiti Bridge* is a real manifesto for both a musician and a musical culture. Although, like his other albums, you feel that more often, the songs are made to stay true to the vision of the former rather than to fit the confines of the latter. It's an effort that seems beyond the pale for nearly anyone else, but normal, of course, for the solitary perfectionist who is Prince. It was this ongoing exploration that ferried Prince from the past to the present, and will take him into the future.

1. New York, 1998. Prince in concert
in The Big Apple.

2. The singer in concert in Detroit, 1985.

406, 407 Prince

3. The multi-talented musician during a guitar solo, 1985.

4. Prince during a 1986 concert in Detroit.

1 and 2. Rio de Janeiro, 1991.
The singer in concert in Brazil.

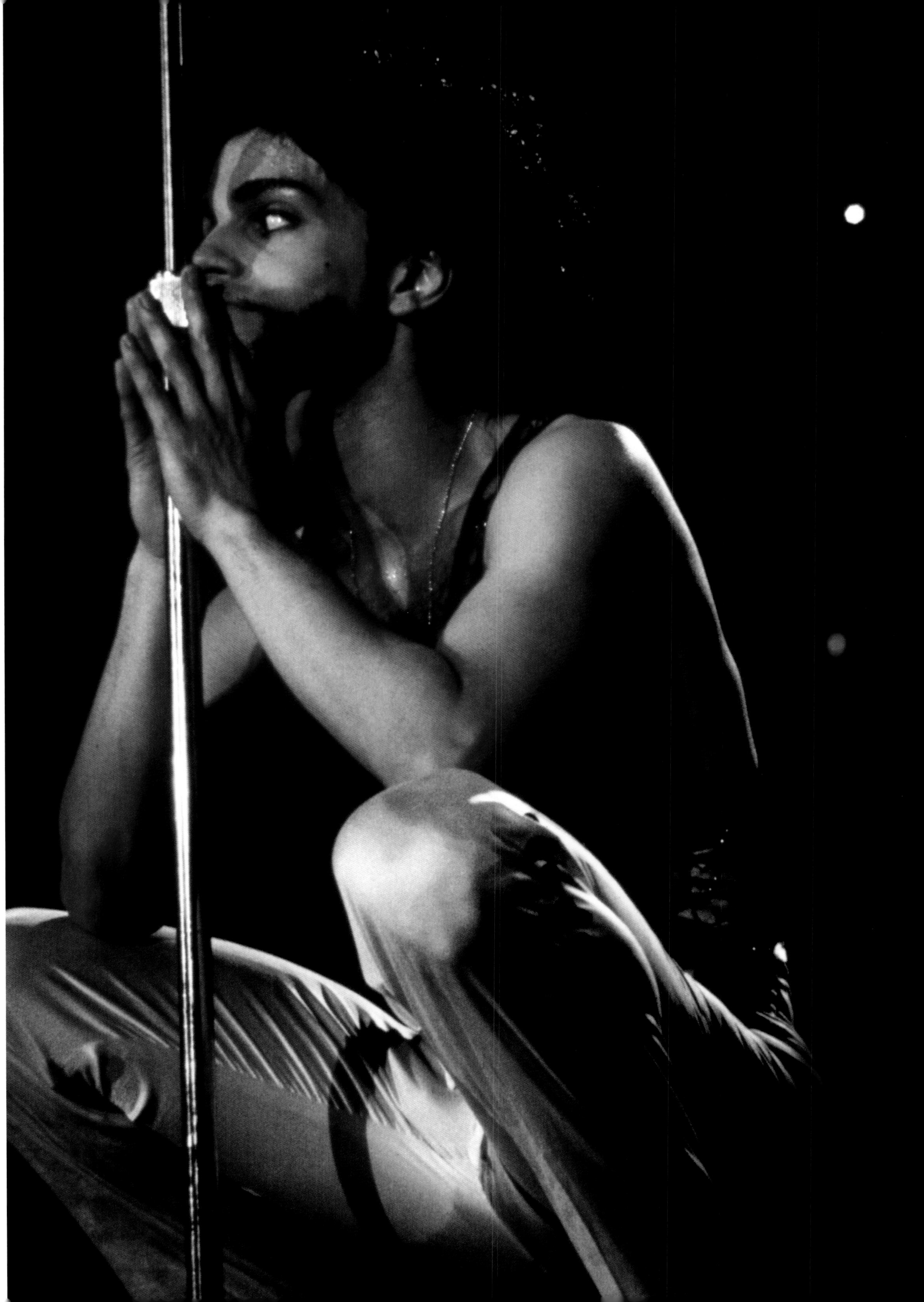

Metallica burst onto the scene in the early Eighties, its musicians little more than teenagers. They brought with them the anger of punk and the speed of youth: *Kill 'Em All is* a truly violent street-rock symphony. They wore plain jeans and their hair was very long (to keep the faith with historic metal that differentiated them from punk). From the start they were grouped with the Heavy Metal New Wave that was raising a storm in the USA and reaching the UK via Germany. This group, however, had something more than just simple nostalgia for the Seventies sound, even if played at three times the speed. They had a crystal-clear social vision that was radical, and in its genre crept into the same bottom-up (up from the asphalt of the great American city hinterlands) social critique that later emerged in grunge. *Master of Puppets* and ... *And Justice For All* are the albums that declare these visions, and the 1991 giant *Metallica* (also known as *The Black Album*) confirmed them and started the band on a new path. They substantially changed their sound and the change was heard even more clearly on the albums that followed. With this evolution, their place in rock history was secured. Metallica taught all the world's new rock groups the fundamentals of modern rock grammar and syntax. Chord changes, managing melody lines, instrument technique – these were the keystones on which Nu Metal and modern rock were built, influencing a diverse array of groups from Evanescence to Linkin Park.

Since then, the quartet that was one of the founders of thrash metal moved on to a more radio-oriented rock genre. Their fans were mostly loyal and their numbers grew: the ranks of metal aficionados that diminished somewhat after the album *Load* were replenished with fans who didn't really come from metal, but from pop/rock.

WHEN ROCK TURNS "HEAVY METAL"

Metallica

411 [SARAGOSSA, 2004] - Metallica's bass-player during the only Spanish concert, held at "The Romeda" stadium, for the "St Anger" album launch.

412 [VIRGINIA, 2004] - Kirk Hammet, Metallica guitarist, during a concert at Norfolk, in Virginia.

413 [NEW YORK, 2006] - Metallica performing during the 21st Rock and Roll Hall of Fame Induction Ceremony.

There were two classic lineups: 1983-1986 James Hetfield vocalist and guitar, Lars Ulrich drums, Cliff Burton bass, Kirk Hammett, guitar. 1986-2001, Jason Newsted replaced Cliff Burton, who was killed in a road accident. The classic albums were: *Kill 'Em All* (Elektra Records, 1983, thrash metal), *Ride the Lightning* (Elektra Records, 1984, thrash metal), *Master of Puppets* (Elektra Records, 1986 thrash metal), *Garage Days Re-Revisited* (EP, Elektra Records, 1987, thrash metal), *...And Justice for All* (Elektra Records, 1988, thrash metal), and *Metallica (The Black Album)* (Elektra Records, 1991, heavy rock).

In 2003 Metallica released *St. Anger*, a very raw album that disappointed old fans and new fans alike.

Oddly enough, and in some ways significantly, there was a legal issue that arose in the late Nineties, involving Metallica and Internet users. Tired of being the most illegally-downloaded act in the Internet (and losing millions of in copyright fees), they were among the promoters of the court case that led to the closure of Napster, the famous site for peer-to-peer MP3 exchange. The case alienated many new-generation fans. It was a bizarre twist of fate for the band, who had started out as rebels and ended up suing the new rebels.

Kurt Cobain, speaking of his past and his approach to songwriting, once said that he was influenced by the things he read, but he was not a slave to them: he didn't think his music and songs were inspired. He explained that his lyrics were fragments of his poetry, just verses from his poems. He always wrote; even before forming the group, he spent a lot of time in his room writing, reading, watching TV, listening to music. Now, simply by uttering "Seattle" we bring to mind some of the best rock to have come out of the United States. And Nirvana is the byword for one of the best expressions of rock to have come out of Seattle. In the early Nineties, the general public caught on to the Seattle phenomenon and discovered that there was a series of groups that were all quite different from one another, but were playing rock with fairly comparable commitment and sound. Bands like Nirvana, Pearl Jam, Mudhoney, Tad, Skin Yard, Screaming Trees, and Alice in Chains populated the local music scene. In Seattle they were playing hardcore, punk, and garage rock, with a high percentage of metal and blues mixed in, the latter two genres filtered by listening to the great Seventies groups, especially Led Zeppelin and Aerosmith. Nirvana, for instance, actually quote these two great influences in a track on *Incesticide* called "Aero Zeppelin," a reference both iconoclastic and affectionate in one fell swoop. It was a fairly common phenomenon for many groups: Green River, the influential Seattle rock band that spawned Mudhoney and Pearl Jam, played rock influenced by The Ramones and The Sex Pistols, derived inspiration from The Lords of the New Church, and covered Bowie songs from the "Spiders From Mars" period. It was a weird family tree that lead right back to the original rock 'n' roll that the early punk wave also referred to when that revolt began in 1976.

KURT COBAIN AND
THE GRUNGE WAVE

Nirvana (Kurt Cobain, vocalist and guitar, Krist Novoselic, bass, Dave Grohl, drums) exploded with Nevermind, still considered a member of an elite group of historic albums. "Smell Like A Teen Spirit" is a rare pearl, one of those pieces that open future horizons. An entire generation saw itself in the neuroses and solitude sung by Kurt Cobain, so the band immediately became a focal point.

Nirvana

415 [INGLEWOOD, 1993] ▲ Kurt Cobain performing with Nirvana in a Los Angeles suburb. The performance went down in history because Cobain, towards the end of the concert, perforated his guitar with a drill and then spun it round his head and wrecked the instrument completely.

The next album was *Incesticide*, a very interesting record: fragmentary and thus to be trailed and explored with some attention, to reconstruct the sound matter that had accumulated from 1988 to 1991, apart from two official albums: *Bleach* and *Nevermind*. Many tracks in this collection are the singles released as mini LPs and compilations by the ultra-famous Sub Pop label that was such an architect of the movement that came to be known as grunge. All Seattle bands recorded for Sub Pop and it was only thanks to the confidence of the label's guru, Jonathan Poneman, that the groups made it at all. *Incesticide* is unrelated to the musical atmospheres and evolutions of *Nevermind*. If the latter was an "easy" album in some ways, because of its greater melodic linearity, *Incesticide* returned the band to its origins – its anger, expressed through the hoarse, often crude, sometimes ingenuous, sound that was nevertheless always sincere and uncompromised – a band battling to emerge. There are legendary tracks like "Turnaround," a Devo song that Nirvana transformed into classic alienated rock, a million miles away from the form but not from the spirit of the original; other songs are more famous because the band sang them in concerts, like "Aneurysm" or "Sliver." Nirvana was a band deeply rooted in the past, but that emerged with a fusion that became a new creation and was unmistakable right from the start. two years after *Nevermind*, Nirvana released *In Utero*, but the only thing that was forming at this point was the end. Cobain always said that if he'd been a Sixties teenager he'd have gone for groups like The Stooges and Blue Cheer, and would have hated Cream as well as most of the Top 40 groups. Nirvana had become what he despised, so he decided to give up. And what a shame he left the world so soon, taking his life after a brief stay in a rehabilitation center that followed an emergency hospitalization after in Rome. His body was discovered April 8, 1994.

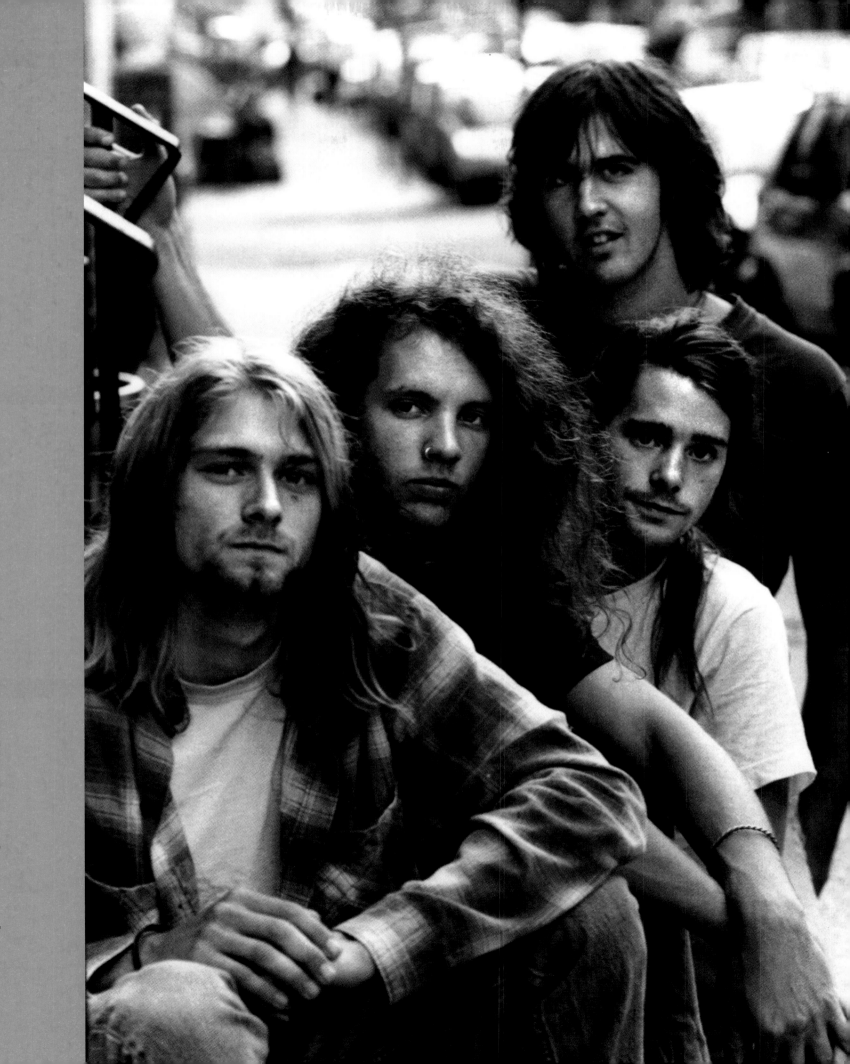

416 AND 417 [NIRVANA, 1989] - Nirvana's line-up posing in 1989, from the left: Chad Channing, Kurt Cobain, Jason Everman and Krist Novoselic.

418-419 [PITTSBURGH, 1991] - A live performance by Nirvana's guitarist.

420-421 AND 421 [TAPING, 1993] - Kurt Cobain while taping
the MTV Unplugged show at the Sony Studios in New York.

Talking of rock Cobain said that if he had been a teenager in
the 1960s, he would have gone for bands like The Stooges
and Blue Cheer, but he would have hated Cream and most of
the other Top 40 groups.
How sad that he took his life so young, when he returned to
Los Angeles, after being admitted to hospital urgently after a
concert in Rome. It was 1994.

Red Hot Chili Peppers' vocalist Anthony Kiedis says that life is beautiful but it

trees and be able to build a better world with his energy, and he'd prefer to die rath

funk-punk band has becoming a reference for the people of rock, and not just in the

By the time they released the album *Blood Sugar Sex Magik*, The Red Hot Chili

of hard work and two broken lives: one lost to tragedy (guitarist and group founde

despair (drummer Jack Irons was so shocked by the loss of his friend that he just

vocalist, and Flea on bass decided to honor their story and their departed friends by

ing the United States in support of the album for nearly two years, recruiting Chad S

When they finally returned to Los Angeles, they spent months shut in a suburban Lo

writing and recording *Blood Sugar Sex Magik*, the album that went on to sell four m

to the single "Under The Bridge," a very personal and contemplative song Kiedis wr

The underpinning to this recording is the quartet's perfect musical timing – o

ahead of their time, until people got older and more sensitive to the group's new sou

always thought that rock as they knew it was no longer enough for their generati

listening to funk, they liked dancing, having sex, feeling good, and more soulful mus

tried to combine their two musical tastes, and their records always pushed in that d

Red Hot Chili Pe

423 [BACKSTAGE, 1989] ▲ Red Hot Chili Peppers, from the left: John Frusciante (guitar), Chad Smith (drums), Anthony Kiedis (vocalist), and Flea (bass-player), posing during a break in a 1989 concert.

424 [BRIGHTNESS] - Anthony Kiedis and Dave Navarro dressed as light bulbs at Woodstock, 1994. The concert was Navarro's debut with the band.

425 [ANTHONY KIEDIS] - The voice of the Red Hot Chili Peppers at Woodstock, 1994.

The Red Hot Chili Peppers introduced crossover music, and that's the main reason for the success of this American band. The amalgam of hard rock or metal music, typical of the white working classes, and funk and rap, which penetrated without distinction all United States classes and communities. From the early Nineties, via *Californication*, recruiting new musicians, the return of old musicians and ongoing world tours, RHCP became a rock legend. RHCP music expressed one of the most "natural" encounters between the two newest seething languages of the Nineties musical scene. The two languages are still around, despite very diversified mingling, for cultural and technical reasons, but the desire for fusion remains. It is the same that inspired Anthrax, Ice T, Public Enemy, and others, with different results.

[LALLAPALOOZA, 1992] - The Red Hot Chili Peppers, with their legendary mix of rock, punk and funk, here the main attraction at the American music festival, 1992.

The band's first compilation is called *What Hits!?*, with 18 tracks from the three LPs and two EPs the released in the Eighties: *The Red Hot Chili Peppers* (1984), *Freaky Styley* (1985), *The Abbey Road EP* (1987), *The Uplift Mofo Party Plan* (1987), and *Mother's Milk* (1989). The album shows how the Red Hot Chili Peppers have gradually approached the core idea of their musical philosophy, a fusion of the white and black music that reside together in the heart of rock, also achieved by working with George Clinton, the talented maestro of Seventies funk.

The Red Hot Chili Peppers are the stars of a real-life story: they went from being a group of friends sharing a passion for music, girls, and fun to being a group of musicians determined to explore directions and new experiences; traumatized by the loss of one of their number and the despair of another, they pushed ahead in the real world and continued to believe in what appeared as almost destiny for them. It was the way to go. Today they are a leading-edge band, with scores of other groups following in their wake, and in their class they are certainly the best.

1. Kiedis during the 21 August 2005 concert at the Borgata Hotel Event Center, Atlantic City, New Jersey.

2. Baring his soul. Another 2005 Atlantic City concert shot: this time the camera focuses on Flea, the band's guitarist.

A lot of water has flowed under the bridge since 1995, the year of the split of Take That, the boy

band that for a few years, broke the hearts of millions of adolescents all over the world, launching a

model that has been repeated and cloned in every market, but never with Take That's overwhelming

media and financial impact. Since then, only Robbie Williams has continued to be successful, slowly but

surely detaching his solo image from that of the "test tube" group that the British record industry

produced to ride the wave of boy-band demand, which was labeled colossal by the marketing gurus.

Now Williams is one of the greats of British pop, with more than 35 million discs sold worldwide. He's a

HOW TO SING IN THE

complete entertainer and adored by audiences of all ages. His secret mission is to last as long as

MOST FAMOUS BOY BAND

possible: on the grapevine they say he's aiming for Frank Sinatra status (or at least Tom Jones).

IN THE WORLD AND

GET TO BE A STAR

Take That & Robbie Williams

431 [THE ORIENTAL TOUCH, 1995] ▲ The five members of the ultra popular band British boy band, Take That, tucking into some oriental-style rice.

Take That were the first British band, after The Beatles, to have four consecutive number one hits, and the first band ever to release eight singles that reached number one in the UK charts within the first week of being released. Their most famous songs were "Pray," "Never Forget," and a cover of the Bee Gees' "How Deep Is Your Love."

These songs are light years away from what Robbie Williams is now recording as a solo artist. He has revealed style and substance that we'd never have expected from the Take That track record. When the pop star described his 2005 album *Intensive Care* he said the tracks evoked nostalgia for Eighties and Nineties songs, as well as the memories associated with them. "Lyrically, this is the best album I've written," he added, "although I do say that before every album comes out." He makes no secret of the fact that his entire career is based "on three movements" – he just mimics Freddie Mercury, Tina Turner, and Mick Jagger.

432-433 [THE IDOL] - Robbie Williams during a 1999 concert.

434-435 [THE WILD MAN OF BRITISH POP] - Robbie performs like a true actor, who fascinates not just with his voice.

437 [MEXICO CITY, 2006] - The singer surrounded by enthusiastic fans during the MTV awards for Latin America.

Williams is the current symbol of British pop, a standard-bearer for an industry that always seems to find new heroes to offer the general public. But he has yet to conquer the American star system, which is a tough mouthful to chew.

[THE KISS] - Williams kisses a fan during the 2006 Mexico City award ceremony.

Their genre is post-Britpop/alternative rock.

London, UK. They are well-known supporters of Amnesty International.

Their music is full of rock melodies and introspective lyrics,

following in the footsteps of Radiohead and Echo & The Bunnymen.

They are Chris Martin, vocalist, piano/keyboards and guitar;

Jon Buckland, guitar, mouth organ;

Guy Berryman, bass, synthesizer, mouth organ;

Will Champion, drums/percussionist, piano and backup vocalist.

Their name has become synonymous with massive success.

FEELINGS

The represent a new generation. They are the new leaders on the scene.

TRANSFORMED

INTO SONG

441 [OSLO, 2000] ⬆ A close-up of Chris Martin, Coldplay vocalist. Behind him the rest of the line-up: Jon Buckland, Will Champion and Guy Berryman.

442 [CONCERT ALMOST ACOUSTIC CHRISTMAS, 2005] - Christmas concert poster for the date at Los Angeles's Gibson Amphitheater, organized and promoted by the KRQQ radio station.

443 [BRIT AWARDS, 2006] - Coldplay on stage at the Brit Awards, London. This was the 26th year celebrating the success of the British record industry: concert proceeds were donated to the British Record Industry Trust.

Coldplay released their first album, *Parachutes*, in July 2000. Apart from critical acclaim, *Parachutes* picked up some criticism for its barely veiled influence from *The Bends* and *OK Computer*-era Radiohead. "Yellow" and "Trouble" got plenty of radio airplay on both sides of the Atlantic and contributed to establishing them as a name. Coldplay went back to the recording studios in October 2001 to start on their second album. Sessions were complex and rumors spread that the band was about to split up, or that the album would be their last, but Coldplay released *A Rush Of Blood To The Head* in August 2002. The album was a huge step forward and the opening track, "Politik," became a the proclamation of the Coldplay philosophy, written just days after the 9/11 terrorist attacks. *A Rush Of Blood To The Head* was a top-selling record, and picked up good reviews from critics. "In My Place," in particular, got Coldplay away from a niche audience and made them known to the great masses, shooting them to superstardom.

444 [HONG KONG, 2006] - Chris Martin during the 13 July 2006 concert in Hong Kong.

445 [BRIT AWARDS, 2005] - Coldplay take the stage at the Brit Awards for "Speed of Sound," voted best British single.

Before getting started, Coldplay loved Echo and the Bunnymen, whose vocalist Ian McCulloch was invited to Coldplay's recording sessions as unofficial studio consultant. Perhaps trying to channel his hero's spirit, Martin wore McCulloch's jacket during recording of "In My Place." Chris Martin and Jon Buckland repaid the favor by guesting on McCulloch's solo album, *Slideling*. Coldplay also perform live versions of "Lips Like Sugar," a Bunnymen hit.

The third Coldplay album, X&Y was released on June 6, 2005, in the UK. The single, "Speed of Sound," drove the album to number one in 28 countries worldwide on its debut. It was a clear signal of the band's planetary popularity. To keep from losing their connection with their core audience, the group played secret concerts in San Francisco, Chicago, Toronto, Boston, and New York City before starting their official 40-date tour. The band played Live 8, in Hyde Park, London, in the summer of 2005.

446, 447 AND 448-449 [SURROUNDED BY FANS] - Coldplay's vocalist, Chris Martin, surrounded by his adoring fans.

In the late Eighties, had a journalist asked Billie Joe Armstrong what he thought he'd do with his punk trio

and his green hair, the answer might well have been on the lines of "f.o.a.d."

16 years later, the punk entered the halls of the classic rock academy, with a classic rock product. In fact,

Green Day won the "Best Group" and "Best Rock Video" awards for "American Idiot" at the MTV Video Music

Awards in Sydney, Australia. They also won the "Best Rock Album" award for *American Idiot* at the 2004

Grammys. On 28 August 2005, the Miami MTV Video Music Awards gave the group acknowledgments in seven

of the eight categories in which it was nominated, including not only the public's award for "American Idiot," but

PUNK IS DEAD.

also Best Video of the Year, Best Band Video, and Best Rock Video for "Boulevard of Broken Dreams."

LONG LIVE PUNK.

Green Day

51 [GREEN DAY, 1997] ▲ The band: from the left, Tré Cool, Billy Joe Armstrong and Mike Dirnt.

53 [LAS VEGAS, 2005] - Green Day's singer Billie Joe Armstrong performing at the Thomas & Mack Center, Las Vegas, in October 2005.

The Green Day story is a long one and it began a long way away. The band got together in Berkeley, California, in 1988, comprising Billie Joe Armstrong, Mike Dirnt, and Al Sobrante (aka John Kiffmeyer), originally called Sweet Children. It was under this name that they released a self-titled EP for an independent Minneapolis label (Skene!). The year after they changed name to Green Day and released *1,000 Hours* for Lookout! Records, an independent Berkeley label, that also had under contract Operation Ivy, a cult band of the time, despite being short lived. Green Day's album *39/smooth* and the *EP Slappy*, both released in 1990, were fairly successful, and the band changed lineup, replacing Al with his drum master, Frank Edwin Wright III, aka Tré Cool. A USA tour in Tré Cool's dad's van followed, and Green Day recorded *Kerplunk!,* which caught the eye of major record companies. Then they left for Europe.

When they got back, they were signed up by Reprise, which unleashed the wrath of many fans, who accused them of selling out. Then came 1994, a fateful year for the group and for the punk rock scene, they released *Dookie*, which became a world chart-topper thanks to MTV, with singles like "Longview," "Basket Case," and "When I Come Around." The album sold 15 million copies and became the best-selling punk record of all time.

The next year the band released *Insomniac*, whose title was inspired by the sleepless nights that Billie Joe suffered after his first son was born: the album didn't equal the success of *Dookie*, selling four million copies. After ten years on the road, 2004 was the year when Green Day recovered the glory of *Dookie* with the album *American Idiot* (from which the single of the same name was taken), a Who-style concept album that achieved critical and public acclaim, due largely to the song "Boulevard of Broken Dreams." The single alone sold three million copies, supported by a moving video that received heavy airplay on MTV, pushing the album to the threshold of eight million copies sold. After "Boulevard of Broken Dreams," Green Day released the singles "Holiday" and "Wake Me Up When September Ends," an emotional tribute to the memory of his father that often moves Billie Joe Armstrong to tears while he is performing it live. "Jesus Of Suburbia," a mini rock opera, lasting eight minutes, is another interesting track from the album.

The Green Day miracle is rooted in hard touring and self-confidence. Even when they veer towards pop from punk in sound terms, they never trade off their critical abilities or their artistic vision. In this respect, they have remained true to their dream.

454-455 [MASSACHUSETTS] - Billie Armstrong and his band play at the opening game of the football season: Oakland Raiders vs New England Patriots, Foxboro.

455 [BRIT AWARDS, LONDON, 2005] - Armstrong spins it on the London stage.

454, 455 Green Day

456 [TRÉ COOL, 2006] - Green Day's drummer, Tré Cool (Frank Edwin Wright III), during the Las Vegas concert promoting "American Idiot."

457 [TOUR, 2006] - Billie Joe points the sky at the end of song.

456, 457 Green Day

458 [MIKE DIRNT, 2006] - Green Day's bass player during a performance.

459 [LAS VEGAS, 2006] - Billie Armstrong points his gratitude to his audience.

Index

Photo credits

AFP/Grazia Neri: pages 265, 345

Esther Anderson/Corbis: pages 84 left, 243

Apis/Sygma/Corbis: page 183

John Atashian/Corbis: page 232

Bill Bailey/Zuma/Corbis: page 284

Bettman/Corbis: pages 68, 69, 70-71, 75, 82-83, 90-91, 92-93, 94, 95, 106-107, 138, 182, 290, 292-293

Jonathan Blair/Corbis: page 181

Karen Mason Blair/Corbis: pages 398-399

Stephane Cardinale/Corbis: pages 364, 365

Javier Cebollada/epa/Corbis: page 411

Patrick Chauvel/Sygma/Corbis: pages 242, 244, 245

Collezione privata: pages 11, 23, 43, 53, 59, 89, 114, 154, 174, 189, 212, 220, 223, 313

Corbis: pages 21 center, 224, 271, 291 bottom, 302-303, 305, 308-309, 347, 348

Corbis Sygma: pages 401, 451

Jason DeCrow/epa/Corbis: page 366

Jay Dickman/Corbis: page 80

Henry Diltz/Corbis: pages 21 top left, 21 bottom right, 82, 102, 120, 125, 128, 129, 137, 146, 191, 192, 193 top, 194-195, 415, 426-427

Epa/Corbis: page 355

Everett/Contrasto: page 133

Ettore Ferrari/epa/Corbis: page 337

Tony Frank/Sygma/Corbis: pages 78, 139

Owen Franken/Corbis: page 304

Gamma/Contrasto: pages 67, 73

Mitchell Gerber/Corbis: page 201

Getty Images: pages 21 bottom left, 31 bottom, 51 top left, 60 bottom left, 63 top, 63 bottom right, 131, 222, 258, 272, 286 left and destra, 287 left, 300, 306-307, 314, 315, 324, 325, 336, 339, 340-341, 358-359, 362, 363, 368-369, 374-375, 376, 377, 379, 381, 396-397, 404, 405, 413, 420-421, 421, 428, 429, 431, 437, 438-439, 443, 444, 445, 446, 447, 448-449, 453, 454-455, 456, 459

Laurent Gillieron/epa/Corbis: page 436

Lynn Goldsmith/Corbis: page 31 top, 41 bottom center, 74, 103, 113, 221, 279, 280, 281, 296, 299, 308, 310, 311, 349, 380

Philip Gould/Corbis: pages 294-295

Douglas Kent Hall/Zuma/Corbis: pages 122-123

Michael Hanschke/epa/Corbis: page 367

Rune Hellestad/Corbis: pages 60 top left, 432-433

Hulton-Deutsch Collection/Corbis: pages 91, 101, 121, 152-153, 167, 188, 289, 291 top

David J. & Janice L.Frent Collection/Corbis: page 93

Steve Jennings/Corbis: pages 41 bottom left, 63 bottom center, 228

Elliot Landy/Grazia Neri: pages 119

Frédéric de Lafosse/Corbis: page 233

LaPresse-Milano: page 166

Rick Maiman/Corbis Sygma: page 406 left

Bruno Marzi: pages 108, 109, 157, 234, 238-239, 329, 385, 434-435, 457, 458

Wally McNamee/Corbis: page 350

Jeff Moore/Zuma/Corbis: page 412

Morell/epa/Corbis: page 371

Tim Mosenfelder/Corbis: pages 179, 273, 277, 285, 287 right

Michael Ochs Archives/Corbis: pages 37, 41 bottom right, 81, 84 right, 117, 134, 135, 153, 218, 266-267

Denis O'Regan/Corbis: pages 170-171, 224-225, 226-227, 227, 253, 257, 302, 391, 392, 393

Thierry Orban/Corbis: page 175

Jacques Pavlovsky/Sygma/Corbis: page 241

Neal Preston/Corbis: pages 31 right, 36 top, center and bottom, 36-37, 41 top, 51 right, 60 right, 77, 85 left and destra, 87, 99, 104, 111, 141, 142-143, 144, 145, 147, 148-149, 160-161, 165, 168-169, 173, 184, 185 top and bottom, 186-187, 193 center and bottom, 196, 198, 202, 203, 204-205, 207, 208-209, 209, 211, 213, 214 left and destra, 215 left and destra, 217, 231, 235, 236, 237, 248, 248-249, 250-251, 255, 256, 259, 260-261, 262, 268-269, 274-275, 278, 282-283, 297, 317, 318, 319, 320-321, 322, 323 top and bottom, 326-327, 330, 332-333, 334 left and destra, 335 left and destra, 350-351, 352, 353, 357, 360-361, 382, 383 top, center and bottom, 389, 394-395, 403, 406 right, 407 left and destra, 408, 409, 423, 424, 425

Aaron Rapoport/Corbis: page 51 bottom left

Reuters Images/Contrasto: pages 63 bottom left, 86, 105, 106, 442, 455

Roger Ressmeyer/Corbis: pages 151, 176, 177, 387, 388

Ron Sachs/CNP/Corbis: page 270

Jacqueline Sallow/Corbis: pages 343, 402

Steve Schapiro/Corbis: pages 114-115

Jerry Schatzberg/Corbis: pages 21 top right, 79, 100, 118, 158, 158-159

S.I.N./Corbis: pages 143, 246, 247, 373, 416, 417, 418-419, 441

Sunset Boulevard/Corbis: pages 126-127

Luciano Viti/Grazia Neri: pages 155, 162, 163, 178, 197, 199, 384

Andy Warhol Foundation/Corbis: pages 96-97, 346

ERNESTO ASSANTE - *Journalist*
music critic for La Repubblica since 1978.

Born in 1958, for almost 30 years he has partnered numerous
Italian and overseas weeklies and monthlies, including *Epoca,
L'Espresso, Rolling Stone,* as well as conceiving and editing the
supplements *Musica*, *Computer Valley* and *Computer, Internet e
Altro* for *La Repubblica.*
He has been a radio presented for RAI and a TV writer for the RAI
and Mediaset networks.
He was director of McLink, Italy's first Internet provider.
He realized and directed the Repubblica.it project.
He was a founder and director of Kataweb.
He has worked with Enciclopedia Treccani to draw up the pop
music entries.
He has written a number of books: *Bob Marley* (Lato Side 1980),
Reggae (Savelli 1981), La Storia del Rock (5 volumes, Savelli
1983), *Il rock e altre storie* (Arcana 1984), *Paesaggio
Metropolitano* (Feltrinelli 1985), *Viaggia la musica nera* (Marcon
1991), *Genesi* (Castelvecchi, 1997), *Il Novecento Americano*
(Einaudi 2004), *La Musica Registrata* (Audino, 2005), *33 dischi
senza i quali non si può vivere* (Einaudi 2007)

**All my thanks must go to Federico Ballanti, whose
collaboration has been fundamental and without whose
assistance this book would never have seen the light of day.**

**The Publisher wishes to thank Bruno Marzi, Maurizio
Ferrara, Attilio Ferrando, Marco Balocco.
Special thanks to Franco Brizi for his precious help in
recovering the albums.**

© 2007 White Star S.p.A.
Via Candido Sassone, 22/24
13100 Vercelli, Italy
www.whitestar.it

Translation: Angela Maria Arnone

All rights reserved. This book, or any portion
thereof, may not be reproduced in any form
without written permission of the publisher.
White Star Publishers® is a registered trademark
property of White Star S.p.A.

ISBN 978-88-544-0281-2

REPRINT:
1 2 3 4 5 6   12 11 10 09 08 07

Color separation: Chiaroscuro, Turin
Printed in China